Alfred B. Starratt

Your Self, My Self
& the Self
of the Universe

LIVING, KNOWING & LOVING · A FAITH
UNITING REASON, SCIENCE & RELIGION

1979

Stemmer
House

PUBLISHERS, INC.
Owings Mills, Maryland

Inquiries should be directed to
Stemmer House Publishers, Inc.
2627 Caves Road
Owings Mills, Maryland, 21117

Published simultaneously in Canada by George J. McLeod,
Limited, Don Mills, Ontario

A Barbara Holdridge book
Printed and bound in the United States of America
First Edition

Library of Congress Cataloging in Publication Data
Starratt, Alfred B
  Your self, my self & the self of the universe.

  "A Barbara Holdridge book."
  1. Religion—Philosophy. I. Title.
BL51.S6259 1979   210   79-9971
ISBN 0-916144-38-0
ISBN 0-916144-39-9 pbk.

YOUR SELF, MY SELF
& THE SELF OF THE UNIVERSE

For all whom I love and for all who love me—
especially for my wife, Anne.
For the Self of the Universe, vividly known to
us in the happiness of our loving.

CONTENTS

INTRODUCTION

I intend this to be a book of religious philosophy for thoughtful people who feel a need to go beyond the traditional myths of past ages. It is not another book about the "Occult." No doubt such books of private revelation and unsubstantiated assertions give great help to many. But I have always thought of "truth" as by its very nature public. Truth is that which is grounded in evidence that can be examined by other qualified observers. To me, "private truth" is a contradiction in terms. So I have written in these pages a way of understanding human experience that is grounded in three kinds of public experience: a scientific construct familiar to physicists in which the nature of reality is seen as variant wave patterns in a single energy field; the testimony of mystics in many cultures and many different times in world history; and the experience of ordinary human beings when they feel a very intense degree of the kind of emotion that we speak of as "love."

I would hold that there is some real possibility that the book is intended for you, simply by the fact that you have it in your hands and have read it thus far. For I think that our free will is one aspect of our existence which, looked at from the other side, can be called "destiny"—that which we did not choose and cannot change.

Perhaps you remember Antoine de Saint-Exupéry's book of

innocent wisdom, *The Little Prince*, in which there was a king who could order the sun to set and the sun would obey him. However, he explained that he was a reasonable king and did not believe in giving unreasonable orders. Hence, before ordering the sun to set, he always consulted an almanac and determined the correct time to give the order for that day of the year. The king chose freely to order the sun to set. The sun obeyed. Yet the sun was not forced and the monarch was not frustrated. It may well be that something like that combination of freedom and destiny happens in the events of your life—including the event of your reading these words. For, as I hope you may be persuaded, All is One and hence All is involved in anything that happens anywhere.

But I'm not going to put you through a lot of mental gymnastics. After years of discussions with groups of adult friends in my library at home, I've had a lot of experience in translating complexities of specialists into the kinds of communication that make sense to non-specialists. So I'll make it as easy as I can when I'm talking about the basic nature of reality. You may have to stop and think and reread the first couple of chapters, embodying the evidence for the Unity— the Self who is Life of our life. From there on it's mostly practical. If everything that exists anywhere in the universe is a differentiation of a single limitless Life, how then should we live?

Notice, however, that the "should" in the above question is not intended to express duty, obedience, or obligation. Words such as "should," "ought," "must" and the like are ways of talking about things that you don't want to do. I agree with the poet Mark Van Doren, who once wrote an essay in which he asserted that a person should never do anything that he really doesn't want to do. He claimed that he had lived by that principle for years; and another great poet, Archibald Mac-Leish, recently wrote of Mark Van Doren that he was "first and foremost and above all a good man, a man famous in his gen-

2

eration for his goodness, for his decency, for his rectitude."* So it would certainly seem to be possible to avoid living with a sense of obligation and yet at the same time to be a very good person.

Doing good, not because you feel you should, but because you really want to, is a way of living that rises spontaneously to the degree that you feel your unity with all that is around you. "Feeling unity" is another way of talking about loving. Perhaps, however, you are one of those who realize that we can't change our emotional life by a single direct act of will. Hence you think it's silly to talk about loving as a basis for good living. But I think I can show you that it is not silly. I can show you, too, that the kind of life that emerges from such "re-membering" will sometimes be unconventional in a creative way that makes a vital and lasting difference to you. When you break out of the rut of the conventional because of a new way of feeling and thinking about the world, you will become part of the answer to human miseries. There will be one more person free to grow in his or her capacity for loving, free to understand and forgive the other, free to bring reconciliation and peace to the places where you live.

Shakespeare was right when he said that ". . . the great globe itself, yea, all which it inherit, shall dissolve, and like this insubstantial pageant faded, leave not a rack behind. We are such stuff as dreams are made on, and our little life is rounded with a sleep." This familiar, beloved land around us is really an event rather than a collection of things. The fair sunlight, the hills, fields, streets, buildings, animals and people, all that we see, hear, touch, taste and smell, yes, and our own bodies with all their sensitivities, all are what the Self of the Universe is doing at various space/time locations within his own limitless reality. He chooses so to act. He may also choose to cease such activity.

* Archibald MacLeish, *Riders on the Earth*, Houghton Mifflin Co., Boston, 1978, page 140.

But in a final sense, the reality is not sticks and stones, brains and bones. All of the countless wonderful visible variations of the activity of the Self of the Universe can fade into the "thin air" of which William Shakespeare wrote without in the least diminishing the One who so acts, any more than the disappearance of a "fist" when I open my hand diminishes the continuing reality of the hand. Because the Self is without boundaries, he is Life of my life, and my identity as conscious personal life continues whether it is manifest as Alfred B. Starratt, or in some other form, or in no form at all. As Emily Brontë wrote more than one hundred years ago, with the clear insight of a poet:

> No coward soul is mine,
> No trembler in the world's storm-troubled sphere:
> I see Heaven's glories shine,
> And faith shines equal, arming me from fear.
>
> O God, within my breast,
> Almighty, ever-present Deity!
> Life—that in me has rest,
> As I—undying Life—have power in Thee!
>
> Vain are the thousand creeds
> That move men's hearts: unutterably vain;
> Worthless as withered weeds,
> Or idlest froth amid the boundless main,
>
> To waken doubt in one
> Holding so fast by thine infinity;
> So surely anchored on
> The steadfast rock of immortality.
>
> With wide-embracing love
> Thy Spirit animates eternal years,
> Pervades and broods above,
> Changes, sustains, dissolves, creates, and rears.
>
> Though earth and man were gone,
> And suns and universes ceased to be,

And Thou were left alone,
Every existence would exist in Thee.

There is not room for Death,
Nor atom that his might could render void:
Thou—Thou art Being and Breath,
And what Thou art may never be destroyed.

Hers was a faith, undoubtedly rising out of an experience of Seeing akin to my own awareness years ago. Faith is another name for belief in which the heart may be more persuaded than the mind. But imagine knowing what Emily Brontë knew—knowing it through persuasion of the mind as well as the heart—knowing it not by blind acceptance of the word of some past authority but because you have considered what modern nuclear physicists are saying; because you have thought of the universal testimony of religious people of intuitive insight in many cultures; because you have thought about the implications of your own most deeply moving experiences of all that is around you; and because you have become aware, through the unity you experience in loving, of the One Life in which we all participate. Imagine knowing that your life is a variant form of the Self of the Universe and knowing it with as much confidence as you know that there is a Law of Gravity active in the universe and influencing the behavior of everything around you at all times in all places! This is the knowing toward which I lead you.

But how does one speak rightly of an infinite, living, personal, creating power? Women will rightly object to calling the One "He." This One transcends all sexual differentiation. But speaking of "He/She" seems awkward, and if I call the One "it," some of my readers may think I'm talking about sheer, mindless force—which I'm not. So I shall use the word "He" as a pronoun and trust your common sense to recognize that my usage is due to the limitations of our language.

As for a name, I can't call him "God" for that calls up

ancient myths and legends that immediately distort in the mind of some readers the reality about which I write. I think of this One as indwelling existence in the same way that my personal life indwells my body. So I speak of Him as the Self of the Universe, and I have written this book to try to help you "re-member" Him—a special kind of "re-membering." This "re-membering" is something like the process one goes through in psychoanalysis. By random communication to a trusted therapist of anything in his consciousness, a patient who has been living in misery finally is able to remember what was dismembered in the early years of childhood. To "dismember" something is to tear apart a living whole. If one has a terrible childhood experience and tears that experience out of the living wholeness of personality by forcing the memory down into the subconscious cellars of the mind, one lives as an emotional cripple until that which was dismembered is re-membered.

A process roughly similar to such dismemberment takes place in each human being as he becomes an individual and takes up his role in the mighty drama of history. We proceed out of the single life of the Self of the Universe and become separate persons by forgetting the primal Unity, letting it slip away into the subconscious. Thus, instead of experiencing this time/space environment as variant forms of activity of the Self, we are aware of a collection of loosely related others and a crowd of competing egos.

But this isn't anyone's fault. On the contrary, the loss of awareness of boundless unity was willed by the Self of the Universe as a necessary condition for the appearance of a space/time, finite universe such as the one in which we live.

The enchanted land of childhood fades. The enchanted land of our adult life together will fade. Yet right here, where you now are, there is a path leading to even greater joy and peace. I go walking with my two dogs. Their excitement shows that they feel the Presence. The trees sense Him too and they are hushed and listening. I stand still, opening all I am to the inflow. A vagrant shred of wind drops down from streams of air high above—a soft, whirling ghost of a breeze, like a breath calling for silence from pursed lips. The wicked witch hides behind yon broad chimney where sits a ragged black crow, her familiar. A squirrel chatters a warning. The sun pushes in among the trees with brighter light, and the contrasting shadows become darker, more vividly present. Good and Evil are dancing now very lightly, hand in hand, on tiptoe. Yet it is Good that always calls the final figure. I am at home in my dearly beloved world. Read my words. Follow me. The path ahead leads to a happy welcoming.

MYTH, VISION AND SCIENCE

The most important things in life are the most difficult to capture in a web of words. The general idea remains in the net, but that which is unique, particular and precious slips through the symbols and is gone.

How easy it is, for example, to say, "I love you,"—how easy, and how inadequate as a witness to the way that one life can be permeated through and through by another life. Plato knew such frustration and his solution to the problem was to tell a myth about a time when human beings were bisexual, each person a unit composed of a complete male and a complete female. These double creatures were so happy that they made the gods jealous. To decrease human bliss the gods caused a deep sleep to fall on all people and then they divided each person into two halves, one half male and the other half female, and they scattered the separated halves so that they were lost to each other. Love is thus the longing for the other half of one's own being. Love is the joy of wholeness that comes with reunion of the two halves of a single life. The myth told by Plato makes no claim to be a narrative of fact. It is simply a way of suggesting intuitive insights that reach beyond our capacity for literal description.

Myth is the inexpressible depth of experience in one person calling to the inexpressible depth of experience in another person. The message is suggested by words and, as in all communication, the meaning of the words rises out of shared experience interpreted through the conventions of a common culture. The meaning of the myth goes beyond the logic of the narrative, however, for the meaning is derived from the wholeness of living experience rather than from rational discourse. It is a way of using words to communicate beyond words. When I hear a myth that is truly meaningful to me, it is as if someone were calling my name, but calling it in such a way that I hear the name of all humanity—the universal flowing through the particular.

It is in this sense that I want to relate the following myth, my own contemporary version of an intuitive narrative told by the campfires of people in ancient India long before the invention of writing. This myth lies behind the ancient Upanishads, but it also suggests ways of understanding reality that are found in modern nuclear physics. The great mystics of all of the various world religions would find it somewhat familiar and certainly congenial. Listen, then, as a child listens to a wonder story. Let the words speak in your heart as well as to your mind:

Before the beginning, the Limitless One was endlessly quiet. Then the One awakened from the sleep of satisfaction. In him the possible began to long for the actual. Restlessness became a measureless pool of energy—pulsing—vibrating. Being and Non-being began to spin as partners in a whirl of delight. Darkness spun away from the figure, leaving a star. Then another star. Between them space was born. One star. Then another. In the interval time was born. From endless to unending stretched space. From boundless to limitless stretched time. Room for a universe. Time for creating.

Form flowed out of starlight. Stars became the womb of creation. In their mightly fire the vibrations of the Dancer of the Universe took on new patterns which were then scattered through space by mighty explosions. Starfire, congealed into stardust, drifted through emptiness. Where we are, stardust slowly gathered into a sphere—incandescent in the gathering; but it slowly cooled and began a living process of evolution. Stardust became earth. Earth became water, atmosphere, vegetation and organisms.

Thus the Infinite One shaped himself into ever more complex and various forms. Because the Divine Dancer is limitless there is no place where he stops and something else begins. The life of all the living is the single life of the Self of the Universe. The changing patterns of all forms of existence are the shapes of his actions. Every experience of every living thing is his experience.

By self-limitation the One differentiated himself and appeared as particular living bodies. In each he became limited knowing. Out of the limitations came competitive struggle, agony and ecstasy. All the pain was suffered by him. All the pleasure was enjoyed by him. Because the one cannot be known without the other, he accepted the suffering to experience the joy. Thus in some of his localized forms the Self of the Universe made himself increasingly sensitive until the drama of creation included inexpressible happiness and its twin, unspeakable pain. In such focal centers of awareness the Self of the Universe had become people.

Around each person the Creating Power placed a veil of unknowing so that the unity of all in the One was hidden. Only thus could the excitement and suspense of his game of becoming a universe be maintained. But the veil was not everywhere of the same density. Here and there, now and then, the One othered himself into people who were sensitive to the unity of all life—Jesus, Moses, Gautama, Lao Tzu, Francis, Eckhart and many, many others. These were aware of the unity of all selves in the Self of the Universe. They lived out of the single source. They spoke of the One. Others, less sensitive, could learn from their words.

Persons were also given the capacity to experience love, which is awareness of one life shared by two—the clue to the realization that one life is shared by all. Thus the sharp and dangerous edges of individualism were softened somewhat by feelings of unity between two and of kinship with the many.

So the One continues to be a universe. In each life he has wonderful adventures until that particular role in the drama dissolves in death and the limited life wakens to the realization that he or she is limitless Life—the author, all the actors, the stage, the scenery, all that ever has been, all that is, all that ever will be of the drama of creation—the single, infinite One who is the Self of the Universe.

As a dancer dances for the joy of dancing, so the One dances the universe out of delight in creative action, and for no other reason.

That is my myth of creation. Its source lies in some very ancient ways of talking about the nature of things. But it is grounded in a contemporary scientific understanding of reality fully as much as in mystical experience and intuitive insight. In non-literal language the myth expresses a modern understanding of the nature of God and of reality as a self-differentiating activity of God. It is a narrative expression of the philosophy called "Panentheism."

Panentheism is derived from three Greek words: *pan* meaning "all;" *en* meaning "in;" and *theos* meaning "god." Panentheism is a philosophy which sees the whole universe as existing *in* God and thus affirms that God is more than all that we can mean by this, or any other imaginable universe. At the same time this philosophy affirms that God is the inner being of everything that exists in the universe. Panentheism means All-in-God-and-God-in-All. It is a philosophy that takes seriously the idea that God is infinite, that is, literally without limits of any kind.

Because our experience of space is without borders, we cannot imagine building a wall around space in such a way that there would be no space on the other side of the wall. In the same way, if God is truly infinite we cannot imagine a boundary where God ends and some kind of non-God substance begins. Hence, as the great Jewish philosopher Martin Buber once put it, God "others himself" in producing the universe. He doesn't "make" a universe as an object "out there" apart from himself. Rather, he "becomes" a universe in one region of his limitless being.

The myth of creation, therefore, expresses a basic philosophical insight into the nature of the relation between God and the universe, consistent with contemporary scientific understanding that energy transactions taking place in the life process of stars are the source of all that goes into the substance of earth and of all that is in, on, and around this planet. The universe evolves from a primal energy field, whether one thinks of that field as moving outward from some prior focal center or one thinks of the field as a steady state of universal, dynamic potential. In either case, the creating power is internal to the process. Existence of forms rises out of formlessness by a process of self-differentiation. Thus the universe is a name for an activity of God in the same sense that a "fist" is a name for an activity of a hand.

Hundreds of years before modern physicists came to the realization that reality is a single differentiated continuum, the same truth was known to the great mystics of many different religions. Their mystical awareness that all things are variant forms of a single divine reality has nothing to do with occult phenomena. Perhaps I can best illustrate the nature of mysticism by telling you about a mystical experience that I had as a boy. Without drugs, without any preparation for it, nor any expectation of any such experience, I went through a timeless period of expanded consciousness in which I became sensitive to a deeper level of reality than is found in our usual human perception of our environment.

In the year 1925 my family lived on a small farm in Danvers, Massachusetts. My father was chief engineer at the Salem Electric Light Company. He had neither the time nor the inclination to work the land, but the farm was a pleasant place for the children in the family—two older sisters and a younger brother besides myself. I was ten years old that summer and thoroughly enjoying my love affair with the world.

One pleasant moonlit night I responded to the call of some inner urge for adventure by climbing out of my bedroom window to the roof of the porch just below. From there, as I knew from many past excursions, it was easy to cross over the top of a couple of intervening sheds and reach the edge of the roof of the big barn. Soon I was up on the ridgepole of that tall building and I sat down feeling that I was at the highest point in all creation. The old farmhouse and the outbuildings were at my back and before me stretched low rolling fields toward a distant stand of trees and then rising hills. The air was clear and still. Moonlight washed out most of the stars and illuminated the scene. Below me Grunt, our pet pig, was making snuffling noises in his pen.

As I sat quietly there on the roof of the barn I began to notice a strange transformation coming over everything I could see. Things were becoming luminous before my eyes. They shone from within, glowing with light in a riot of colors that continuously increased in intensity. It was as if the grass of the fields, the brown fences, the red barn that belonged to our neighbor, the white walls and green roof of our own house when I turned to look back—as if they all were made of stained glass with sunlight shining through them.

As this inner light grew brighter I noticed that it pulsed with a steady rhythm that appeared to me to be the beating of some gigantic heart, as if it were the life-throb of the Self of the World. The scene became a living, scintillating dance of glory—everything beautiful and everything just right in relation to everything else. The very darkness of the distant trees and hills became shining purple and blue.

Then something more strange happened. While still retaining awareness as an individual, the sense of "me" at a fixed location in space and time expanded into less limited conscious perception. I can try to suggest what happened by saying that there was a shift of identity from the self of an observer to all that was there to be observed. Instead of seeing that living light, I became the light. It was seeing without any specific person doing the seeing from any particular perspective. The whole circle of the horizon was before my eyes simultaneously.

My personal life became universal life. The rhythm of the luminous pulse beat was the surging rhythm of my own vital processes which had become identical with inner shaping and sustaining power of all creation. I could feel directly the variant urges, strivings and relationships of the different forms of the one limitless life. I felt in a tree its love for the earth and air; the holding-on of fence posts; the grass reaching toward the light; all things gathered and held in the supporting embrace of earth. I was also sensitive to conflict among the various forms, where life struggled with life and one kind of existence was absorbed into another kind. But the opposing tensions was experienced as one hears dissonant chords in great music which add to the beauty as they are resolved into harmony.

How long the experience lasted I cannot say, but eventually the process reversed itself. My conscious awareness took up again the perspective of a particular location on the roof of the barn. The light of glory faded. My seeing became natural human vision again and I had returned to the sensory limitations of a little boy with an aching bottom from sitting for some unknown length of time on the ridgepole of the barn roof.

So what do you do with the most perfect experience of your life? No one had to tell me that nothing like this had ever happened to anyone I knew. They'd say I was dreaming—maybe even that I'd had some kind of crazy fit. Everyone I knew would explain it in such a way as to reduce it to shameful oddity. Members of my family already complained often enough that I was a strange lad, ". . . always has his head stuck in a book instead of going out to play with the other children. And when he does go out it is mostly by himself—living in some dream world of make-believe characters out of his books."

On a high hill in Danvers there was a group of old red brick buildings that everyone called The Insane Asylum. You were locked up there if you were different from everyone else. So I kept my experience to myself. It wasn't until years later, after I had learned of mystical experiences that happened to other people, that I told anyone about what had happened to me that summer night in 1925.

There are a few events in my lifetime that return vividly to present awareness at the slightest stimulus. Only this one event has companioned all my days. The memory goes with me in the same way that thirst goes with a thirsty man. He may be completely occupied with other things and paying no conscious attention to his thirst, but all of his conscious experience takes place within the atmosphere of his needing a drink. He is aware of thirst even while he is concentrating on other matters. If any choice is offered to him in any way related to the possibility of liquid refreshment, his latent desire will press forward to guide his decision. Through all the years of my life I have been guided like that by my brief boyhood awareness of reality. The memory led me into the study of philosophy and then into religion, where my interest was drawn toward the great mystical religions of the Orient. That boyhood experience brought me eventually to China where I taught at Huachung University in Wuchang up to, and through the first year of, the new Communist Government. I returned to the United States eager to study the new conclusions of physicists in their understanding of reality after Albert Einstein had corrected the dualistic, clockwork image of the universe invented by Isaac Newton. I have been excited, but not surprised, to discover that studies in nuclear physics have dissolved the old materialism in a vibrating field of energy. The ineffable unity of my boyhood mystical experience was finding confirmation in the work of scientists who were active on the outer edges of our new knowledge of nature.

Albert Einstein was the first scientist to conceive of the universe as a single field—one substance differentiated into all the countless forms of existence. In some of its forms it relates to our human sensory apparatus in such a way that we speak of it as energy. In other forms this same dynamic power affects our senses in such a way that we call it matter. The difference, however, is a difference in the activity of a single substance. In a similar way we speak of H_2O in one of its forms as steam, which is an invisible gas, while in another of its forms we call it ice, which is a visible and tangible solid. As steam and ice are variant forms of water, so matter and energy are variant forms of one, active, self-differentiating substance that is the only ultimate reality of this universe. As a whole and in all of its parts the universe is various forms of activity of this one stuff. It is without beginning and without end. It is to space as water is to an ocean. It is everywhere present, everywhere active in continuous changes of form at various space/time locations.

Einstein's famous equation, $e = mc^2$, in which "e" represents energy (in ergs), "m" represents mass (in grams) and "c" represents the speed of light (in centimeters per second), has caught and held our attention, if for no other reason than the enormous quantities of energy it shows to be present in matter. Regrettably the quantitative aspect of the equation tends to override in our minds the ontological aspect. Since the "c^2" in the equation represents only a number to express conversion of energy to mass, or mass to energy, we can ignore the quantitative measurement and simply notice the monumental fact involved in the statement that $e = m$! Energy *is* mass and mass *is* energy, and the difference between the two is only one of temporary state!

Energy and matter are variant forms of activity of a single substance, just as electromagnetic radiation that stimulates the organs of sight appears a light of one color when it vibrates at a wavelength of 3,000 angstroms, and as a light of quite another

16

color when it vibrates at a wavelength of 6,000 angstroms. When the creating substance behaves in one way we speak of it as matter. When it behaves in another way we speak of it as energy.

It appears contrary to common sense to say that every individual thing in the whole universe, without a single exception, is a variant form of one primal stuff. It is difficult to believe that the human brain, a concrete block, sunshine and rose petals are all one substance, for they appear to our sense as not at all alike. Fortunately, however, there is a very common phenomenon known to all of us which, by analogy, may help us to comprehend the meaning of the post-Einstein view of reality. I refer to the world that we view in the picture tube of a television set.

When we turn on the set, a world very like our own daily environment appears on the TV screen. It is a world that contains all the familiar variety of things we commonly experience: rocks, trees, houses, animals, people and all the rest. The television world is a copy of our daily environment in two dimensions rather than three. Yet we know that the television world in all of its variety is a manifestation of various patterns of energy vibration in a single, seamless field of broadcast energy.

In modern scientific understanding our world is like that: a primal vibrating field of energy that shapes itself into all the various forms of existence. The One becomes many while still being one, just as the single energy field sent out by the broadcasting station becomes the endlessly varied two-dimensional world when passed through the circuits of a TV set. Indeed, one could say that the circuitry of our sensory nervous system is roughly similar in function to the circuitry of the TV set. The world of our common perception appears in consciousness as a result of the interaction of our senses and the energy field that is the dynamic shaping power behind all phenomena.

Another analogy that may help us to understand that the universe is a continuum of variety in unity comes to mind in the way a whirlpool exists within the flowing water of a river.

Whirlpools in a river have a definite temporal history. They begin as a slight surface disturbance, and grow larger in a circular pattern of motion, then diminish and disappear. The duration of such a vortex may be brief, but the form is definite. One could photograph a particular whirlpool and give it a name. Yet the whirlpool is not something different from the river. It is simply a temporary pattern of motion of the river water. It is a differentiation within a continuum; a variation existing within one continuous moving substance.

This is the basic ontological meaning of Einstein's equation. Because $e = m$, we no longer need to submit to the mechanistic materialism of Newtonian physics. The universe is not made up of two kinds of stuff—hunks of matter being pushed around by energy. And God is not an absentee clockmaker who put the universe together, wound it up and then went off on other errands. Everything we know points to the realization that the universe was not put together from the outside as if by some structural engineer. Rather, it evolves from the inside, so to speak. It is self-differentiating. At countless separate space/time locations the endless ocean of primal energy moves into particular patterns of activity, just as river water flows into patterns of waves and whirlpools, and each of these patterns becomes for us a distinct "thing" that can be observed and named.

Each and every one of us, in our *total* personal existence, are, like all other forms of existence, particular patterns of activity of the infinite primal energy field. We are kin to rocks and stars, earth and sea, the smallest midge and the mightiest whale. Our existence is by its very nature ecological. We are what the whole universe is doing at our location in time and space.

Such sensitivity as Francis of Assisi felt for "Mother Earth," "Brother Fire," "Sister Water," as well as for birds and beasts, was not mere sentimentality—an emotion disproportionate to the object that called it forth. In the light of our contemporary scientific knowledge of the kinship of all forms of existence, it is people like St. Francis who are in touch with reality, and it is the impersonalists who are blinded by their dogma. The scientist is committed to methods of investigation that make it impossible for him to consider his feelings of kinship with others as evidence of the nature of reality. As husband, lover, father or friend he knows perfectly well that a person is more than a bio-chemical system. But when he is behaving as a scientist he cannot admit what he knows as a human being.

The scientific understanding of that which is ultimately real is true so far as it goes, but it is important to remember that the primary rule of the scientist is that he will deal only with that which he can observe in the world outside of his skin, the environment on the far side of his sensory apparatus. His research is confined to what is called the "objective" aspect of human experience; to the world "out there" in the common area of public perception where procedures and observations can be shared and confirmed. Scientific methodology thus excludes from the body of scientific knowledge the given fact of personal conscious awareness.

In the scientific meaning of the word, "knowing" is a transitive verb that requires independence of subject and object. "I," over here, know something that is "not-I" over there. But in knowing our self-existence as personal conscious awareness, subject and object are identical. The existence of subjective personal consciousness can be described by the simple statement, "I know," for the condition of conscious awareness is accurately designated by a simple statement that there is knowing, without specifying any particular content, just as one might say, "I see," without specifying what one sees. The observer cannot be the object of his own observation any more than he can eat his own mouth, kiss his own lips, or look into his own eyes. Consciousness can never be known as an object, for consciousness is that which does the knowing. So if, as scientists, we arbitrarily decide that only what can be known as an object is real, if we limit knowledge to objective knowledge, then we assert that there is no such thing as personal consciousness. There is only the groove on the record followed by the needle that produces the music. There is no musical genius who composed the music on the recording, for he appears nowhere in the record player. Hence it is no surprise that the scientist in his professional stance is an impersonalist. For him the universe is a mindless, differentiated continuum of energy transactions.

When studying a human being, for example, a physicist will bring into his description only those aspects of our existence that can be known from the viewpoint of an external investigator using the evidence of his senses. In our day he would have available to him a wide variety of apparatus which vastly increase his capacity to perceive and record the phenomena he examines. Yet in all of his research he remains an outside observer studying the evidence available to his senses. Using an electroencephalograph the scientist could detect waves of electronic energy inside your skull. He could note the fact that these vibrations of energy are related to certain states of your body, but he could have no sensory perception of the fact that what he sees as waving lines of light in the oscilloscope of his apparatus are known to you in your personal awareness as thoughts, memories, hopes, fears, loves, all the rich variety of personal conscious life. At your space/time location the single, limitless ocean of energy has shaped itself into a limited pattern of vibration and movement that appears to the external observer as matter charged with energy, and that in subjective awareness is experienced as personal consciousness. Because personal consciousness cannot be observed, the scientist, *qua* scientist, ignores it—even though this involves the paradox of a person deciding that persons do not exist.

Within the limits of scientific methodology the physicist is correct in saying that you are a particular conformation of energy/matter. Within the undeniable reality of subjective awareness you know that you are personal conscious life. These are two ways of knowing a single reality. You exist as a differentiation of the infinite continuum of energy/matter, and within that differentiation your self-experience is that of personal life. It follows that the primal, dynamic, creating substance that can appear to our senses as either power or particles contains personal life. Permeating, and completely one with, the whirling dance of vibrations that is your body there are vibrations of another frequency which follow a pattern that is your conscious self.

To appreciate fully this complex unity we must break away from our habit of thinking in gross geometrical terms. Our personal life is not "in" our body in the same way that the contents are "in" a box. Rather, the relation of the body and the conscious self is similar to the relation between clear, colorless sunlight and the colors of the rainbow. The rainbow colors are all "in" the sunlight, as one can easily see by passing sunlight through a glass prism. So personal life is in the matter/energy process that is designated as your body.

You are personal. You exist as a variant form of the single limitless continuum of primal substance in the same way that a wave is a variant form of the surface of the ocean. What you are the universe is. *So the endlessly active continuum of being is personal.* Doubtless, in the vastness that is beyond our limited powers of comprehension, the continuously active primal being is much more than all that we could mean by the word "personal." But it is not less.

Here, then, we have the new meaning of the word "God." The word designates the boundless, dynamic continuum that shapes itself into all forms of existence, and that includes conscious personal life as an intrinsic quality of its being. It is important to remember, however, that this divine Self who is one with the universe and who also far transcends the universe is not the same as the limited anthropomorphic deity of the Bible. In this new dimension of understanding, when we speak of God as "he," we are simply following the grammatical rules of the English language in which there is no pronoun that refers to a person without endowing that person with a specific sexual identity. We use the pronoun "he" only as a way of reminding ourselves that the continuing process of creation is guided and controlled by something more than blind chance, something more than the rigid determinism of mechanical cause-and-effect relationships, something more than an octillion megaton volts of mindless electricity. Similarly, when we speak of God as "the One," or "the Creating Power," we are not adopting the impersonalist viewpoint of orthodox scientific dogma. Rather, we are reminding ourselves that our understanding of God is not to be identified with the supernatural old man in the sky. We shall often speak of God as "the Self of the Universe." Such a term suggests a personal being who is the inner life of all that exists.

Having been led by science to the realization that the universe is a continuing action of the Creating Power in the same sense that a fist is a continuing action of a hand, we are now in a position to see that the linear reasoning of the physical scientist tends to confirm the holistic, intuitive awareness of the mystic, whether he or she happens to be Christian, Hindu, Buddhist, Sufi, or any other religion. Knowing that contemporary science sees the universe as a single differentiated continuum, we are not surprised that mystics universally testify that as a result of their experience they know themselves to be one with the Self of the Universe, who is the living, shaping and sustaining power in all forms of existence.

My contemporary version of the Myth of Creation, which I told at the beginning of this chapter, makes an educated and intuitive guess at the relationship between the self of a human being and the Self of the Universe, by saying that in you the One chooses to assume the state of a limited focal center of consciousness. Speaking in metaphors I said that he draws a veil of forgetfulness around each person as in each he takes on a particular role in the drama of creation. We shall see that such self-limitation is the necessary condition for the One to experience all the drama and adventure of space/time living. But the veil is not equally opaque around everyone. Mystics are those persons who have experiences that make them utterly certain that their personal self is identical with the Self of the Universe.

A good example of such awareness of the identity of the human self and the infinite Self runs through the writings of the great Christian mystic, Meister Eckhart. In his twenty-third sermon, to cite but one passage, he says, "The eye by which I see God is the same eye by which God sees me. My eye and God's are one and the same—one in seeing, one in knowing, one in loving."

Few people have such vivid awareness of the identity of the personal self and the Self of the Universe. Yet there are vast numbers of people who are not altogether alien to such mystical experiences. The affirmations of unity between the limited self and the infinite Self stir in them a kind of paradoxical forgotten memory. It is like being certain that we know a particular name of a person and we feel, so to speak, a blank space in our mind where that name fits, but at the moment we cannot recall what it is. In such people there is an intuitive openness toward the One while at the same time the One is hidden from the light of their analytical reason.

Modern studies of the psychology of consciousness show that the two hemispheres of the human brain are centers of two kinds of knowing: the left hemisphere being the center of analytical, rational thought, and the right hemisphere being the center of intuitive, holistic awareness. In these terms we people of American and European culture tend to function in terms of our left brain, while our right brain is poorly developed. We are masters of verbal, linear reasoning, but largely insensitive to our own intuitive powers. The technological orientation of our culture does not tend to be conducive to the nurture of mystics. Yet something stirs beyond the veil of analytical reasoning when we hear what the mystics have to say. Something limitless calls our name, and all the great world religions have evolved from responses to that call as modified by the wide variety of cultural milieus.

The impersonalist who views the world as a collection of separate objects assembled by chance is like a man standing in a room that is illuminated by several candles placed on a shelf in front of him. This man believes that he is experiencing light in the only way that it can be experienced—as flowing from several independent sources. If, however, he turned around, he would see only a single field of illumination in which all the different lights coalesce in a single luminous field. The mystic is a person who has turned around. He experiences the Unity that lies within all multiplicity; the Sameness within all differences; the limitless Creating Power within all various forms; the Self of the Universe manifest as our unlimited environment. The mystic can say, with Jesus of Nazareth, "You are the light of the world." The mystic can also say with Jesus, "I am the light of the world." For there is only one light and each of us is a form of the limitless luminosity.

Science and mysticism are complementary ways of knowing the Self of the Universe. Neither gives a complete account of reality. One fills in what the other leaves out. The scientist comes to knowledge of the One, who is also the many while still remaining one, by a process of impersonal, theoretical understanding of objective, empirical evidence. The mystic comes to knowledge of the same reality by his experience of personal identity with the One. Each completes what is left unsaid by the other.

Most people are neither physical scientists nor persons of vivid mystical experience. Hence their knowledge of the Creating Power comes to them secondhand through the reports of others. But the Self of the Universe has not left himself without evidence of his reality that is accessible to the common run of humanity. The clue to the knowledge that all of us participate in one infinite life lies in our hearts. Most of us do not recognize it for we fail to realize what is implied in our feelings. As we shall see, almost everyone has a small but direct acquaintance with the One in our personal experience of loving. Such awareness becomes doubly important when we consider the death of Yahweh, the biblical god.

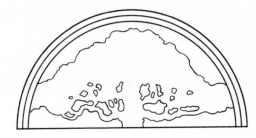

FROM YAHWEH TO NOTHING

High above the Yangtze River valley, in the Kuling Mountains, there is a cemetery where the gravestones bear witness in uncommon quantity to a particularly poignant kind of grief. The Bible verses and pious sentiments on these markers are about what one would expect in a graveyard maintained by foreign missionaries for the burial of their dead. It is the dates on the stones that tell of suffering: "Henry—Born 1881 —Died 1886." "Mary—Born 1892—Called Home 1895." "Rachel—Born 1903—Died 1905." They are almost all like that, the graves of children whose small bodies had been carried up to this last resting place from the raging heat and fevers of the steaming valley below. The fatal illness started often with a rash called "Prickly Heat," which was followed by boils, followed by other infections and death. The quiet plot of land in China is haunted by the heartbreak of all those parents who left in that cemetery a most precious part of their flesh and blood. The sacrifice of children is the most ancient proof of total devotion to a living god.

One remembers the stench of burning flesh in the fires that burned before statues of Moloch. One recalls how Abraham lifted the knife over the body of his only son. These missionaries to China were not as direct in their sacrifice but the effect was the same. Instead of returning to the healthier climate and better medical care of America, they chose to stay in China where their children died. Their devotion bears silent witness to their complete confidence that they served a living god.

The price these missionaries paid to serve their god seems doubly tragic when one remembers that at some time during the next fifty years the biblical god died. No monument marks his burial place. His death took place in the minds of people rather than in the world outside of our heads. However, if there were such a marker it might read as follows:

Here lies Yahweh
The God of all Bible Believers.
Born: Before the Beginning
Died: In the 20th Century of the Christian Era
god is dead. Long live God.

Friedrich Nietzsche was the prophet who foretold this death. In section 125 of *The Joyful Wisdom* a madman proclaims the terrible vision, and no one pays attention. "Do we not now wander through an endless Nothingness?" asks the psychopath as he feels the consequences of the death of god. The question is not heard because the vision is personal, rather than general. The public accepts only what can be seen, tasted, felt or thought about by everyone. It is a book of the late nineteenth century.

Then came the great migration to a new world. A whole generation of people found themselves transported from the world of muscle power to the world of mechanical and electronic technology. Only the metaphor of migration is strong enough to express the changes we experienced during the twentieth century. We have been through more radical cultural transformation in a single lifetime than has been known in the whole history of the human species. We remember the horse and wagon but have seen men land on the moon. We were earthbound yet have seen pictures of our planet taken from outer space. We once learned the news from hometown gossip and now we are part of a global village through instant electronic communication.

Naturally we carried our old biblical god with us to the new world, but as the years went by he seemed more and more a quaint curiosity in the new environment. His three-story universe, with Heaven above and Hell below, was no longer credible in the space age. His fierce partisanship for a chosen few and his merciless disregard for all other people became more and more distasteful in a place where human concern was increasingly universal in outreach. His demand for worship and for unquestioning obedience to arbitrary commands appeared dictatorial as people took more seriously the ideals of democracy. An awareness of the immorality of manipulation developed among a psychologically sophisticated people who grew uncomfortable with the way the biblical god used threats of eternal torture in Hell and promises of bliss in Heaven to manage the lives of believers. His demand for blood sacrifice as the price of his forgiveness, and then his limitation of that forgiveness only to those who believe certain theological propositions inspired revulsion.

In the new world of the twentieth century the image of the biblical god came to be seen as more and more primitive—a relic from a very different past. His mental construct was like the reconstructed skeleton of a gigantic flesh-eating dinosaur. Some memory embedded deep in the body brings shivers at the sight of those terrible jaws even though the species is no longer a threat to our existence. The biblical god continued to provoke emotion in a similar way and we maintained ceremonies in his honor, though as the years went on they felt more and more like celebrations in memory of an honored ancestor. We overlooked flaws of character and emphasized the wonder of past deeds.

The attitude was different among children born in the new world. They had never lived in the old country. The only environment in which they had lived was factually incompatible with the world of the biblical god. For them he was a fictional character out of books of ancient mythology as were Jupiter or Apollo. Despite family attempts to indoctrinate them in the old religion, they ignored it as soon as increase of years gave them some degree of independence.

So it was that when some theologians in the middle of the twentieth century repeated Nietzsche's assertion that "God is dead," the news provoked discussion but not much surprise. We had come a long, long way from those small stones in the Kuling Mountains marking the graves of missionaries' children. That small cemetery in China lies on the far side of a chasm in time. The gravestones there are monuments not only to lost children but also to a complete world-view that has vanished from external existence and is preserved only in the mental world of words. The time is long past when missionaries were willing to sacrifice their children, if necessary, to fulfill the sacred obligation to convert the heathen.

Indeed, no one talks about "missions" any more—at least not seriously in the standard-brand churches. What was called "The Missionary Offering" has become the amount set aside in the parish budget "for work outside of the local church." Each member used to decide for himself how much of his personal pledge would go to "Missions." Now some official board of the local church makes that decision. Not trusting the zeal of individuals, they allocate some portion of the total parish budget to outside work. Where generosity once was motivated by enthusiasm for the cause, church leaders now depend on thoroughly secular techniques of fund-raising which have been given the sweet order of piety by baptizing them as "Stewardship."

The fact is that most people who claim to be Christians would not give a dime to convert foreigners to their version of Christianity. This is perhaps the strongest indication that at some time between the dates on those Kuling gravestones and the middle of the twentieth century, the biblical god had died.

"Do we not now wander through an endless Nothingness?" Nietzsche's madman asked the crowd in the marketplace, but they ignored the question. The indifference of the multitude is also part of Nietzsche's prophecy of the death of god and this part of the prophecy also is fulfilled. Twentieth-century crowds in modern marketplaces, busy with buying and selling the countless fascinating products of the new technology, are deaf to the madman's philosophical question. Only the very sensitive feel the emptiness of the human situation after the death of god. In one of his short stories Ernest Hemingway wrote, "Our Nothing who art in Nothing, Nothing be thy name . . ." The late Loren Eiseley, poet and paleontologist, had a particularly poignant sensitivity to the barren human environment. Because he loved the world, it saddened him to think of it as a most precious and fragile construct, a momentary beautiful order doomed to dissolve into chaos. Feeling the flow of time from darkness to darkness he included in his autobiography a few remembered lines of poetry that are the continuing shadow of his artistic perception:

> behind nothing
> before nothing
> worship it the zero . . . *

Fathered by certain assumed basic continuities of electronic activity and mothered by fifteen billion years of time, with chance acting as midwife, the present state of existence evolved as a mindless construction, a happening, an accidental event. The beauty of this blue jewel hung in space and all that flies, runs, swims or grows on its surface expresses nothing eternal or intentional in reality. The new orthodoxy demands an impersonal view of the nature of things. In his most recent book on the evolution and physiology of the human brain Dr.

*Loren Eiseley, *All the Strange Hours*, Charles Scribner's Sons, New York, 1975, p. 8.

Carl Sagan writes: "My fundamental premise about the brain is that its workings—what we sometimes call 'mind'—are a consequence of its anatomy and physiology, and nothing more. . . . both because of a clear trend in the recent history of biology and because there is not a shred of evidence to support it, I will not in these pages entertain any hypotheses on what used to be called the mind-body dualism, the idea that inhabiting the matter of the body is something made of quite different stuff called mind."*

Dr. Sagan is correct in his statement that the recent history of biology exhibits a clear trend toward interpreting "mind" as a general name for the functioning of the brain. There is no scientific evidence of a ghost inhabiting and operating the human machine. Biologists tend to see man as an unimaginably complex biochemical system, a chance arrangement of matter that happens to have some temporary capacity for survival as an identifiable process. Man is not a spirit that has or possesses a body. He *is* a body.

Having exorcised the ghost from the machine, the modern impersonalists are fascinated by the ways in which electronic computers can be made to duplicate certain of the functions of the brain. Isaac Asimov, the learned interpreter of contemporary science for the community of well-educated non-specialists, expresses a general attitude of scientists in the following paragraph:

"Attempts to mimic the mind of man are as yet in their infancy. The road, however, is open and it conjures up thoughts which are exciting but also in some ways frightening. What if man eventually were to produce a mechanical creature, with or without organic parts, equal or superior to himself in all respects, including intelligence and creativity? Would it replace man, as the superior organisms of the earth

* Carl Sagan, *The Dragons of Eden*, Random House, New York, 1977, p. 7.

have replaced or subordinated the less well-adapted in the long history of evolution?"*

Only one who conceives of intelligence as the physical functioning of a brain could imagine building an electronic device superior in performance to all activities of the human mind. A complex set of molecules assembled by chance, surviving by fortunate adaption to circumstances in a continuously changing environment, puts together a still more complex set of molecules with even greater survival value! Brain creates Superbrain! It is the stuff of which science-fiction is made.

But dualism dies hard. The language of the most orthodox of the impersonalists betrays them. Mr. Asimov tells us that the creation of Superbrain would be a "victory of intelligence over nature." Intelligence *versus* nature? Doesn't the process consist only of complex molecular structures producing more complex molecular structures—a monistic rather than a dualistic process? Whence comes this non-natural stuff that hopes to win a victory over nature?

Isaac Asimov probably would correct his statement by calling it a slip of the tongue. His words ran on beyond the intent of his mind. But the verbal error serves to remind us of the curious way in which scientists can become forgetful of their own existence as observers and theoreticians. They like to describe the world in an impersonal way—the world *as it is*, so to speak—quite apart from any human experience. In their passion for objectivity they forget that there is in reality no such thing as an observation made without any observer, or empirical evidence that is unrelated to people's capacity to make judgments on the basis of their sensory perceptions. The personal element is there in the impersonalist description of reality, but it is not found in the description because the personal is that which is doing the describing.

* Isaac Asimov, *Asimov's Guide to Science*, Basic Books, Inc., New York, 1972, p. 860.

We shall return to this habitual forgetfulness later in these pages. Here it is enough to remind ourselves that in the realm of Nothingness after the death of god people find no trace of personal life in nature. We are taught to believe that persons who so describe nature are equally impersonal since they can be subjected to objective observation and analysis which shows them to be only complex arrangements of material substance. Our loving, our striving, our tears and laughter, our sense of awe before the wondrous beauty of this dear earth, all of it is an evanescent glow around chemical reactions.

Loren Eiseley left out the middle term in his cry of dereliction. "Behind nothing," he wrote. "Before nothing," he added. The middle term is, "Here and now nothing." But he couldn't say it. He cared too much to be able to recite wholly the creed of scientific impersonalism.

Most people care too much. Not all the time. When immersed in the crowd or occupied with products of the new world they can ignore the emptiness of the impersonalist universe after the death of god. But there are times when the part about "nothing in the here and now" is an unbearable assertion. A person falls in love, or cherishes a child, or says goodbye beside an open grave, and the demand that there be something more than a chance arrangement of matter becomes a silent agonized cry that vibrates through the whole of his existence. Intellectual integrity demands acceptance of the courageous honesty and precise reasoning of scientists, but something in the right brain, the intuitive, holistic part of the cortex, insists that an essential part of reality has been left out of the impersonalist description.

Albert Szent-Gyorgyi, winner of two Nobel Prizes for his work in physics and biology, referred to the missing element in a lecture he delivered at the Symposium on the Relationship between the Biological and Physical Sciences, at Columbia University. "I have often been reproached," he said, "for being a vitalist, mysticist, obscurist, and teleologist while the real situation was [to my opponents] clear and simple, there being a complete interdependence between structure and function. Since every function must have its underlying structure which must be of physical nature, all we have to do is to apply physics to structure. This may be so, but all the same, I feel we must be careful with this interdependence because we don't know how many unknowns our equations still contain. Certainly there is such interdependence, as there is complete interdependence between the needle of your gramophone and the groove of your record; and once the needle follows the groove, your victrola must produce the sound it does. All you have forgotten is only Beethoven or Bach, whose music you might have been playing, and without whose genius your gramophone would be useless. Of course, Bach and Beethoven too were built of macromolecules, but, all the same, we do well to keep our reverence before their genius, which is still far beyond the possibility of detailed physical analysis. Such a speechless deep reverence and amazement before the wonders of nature is the main result of my half a century's 'poaching,' and if I were to sum up my summary now, I would do it in Shakespeare's words, saying: "There are more things in heaven and earth, Horatio, than are dreamt of in your philosophy."*

Without denying the validity of the scientific equations, we shall be concerned here with the "unknowns" that are missing from them; with the part of our human experience that is often ignored when one is being scientific. In the metaphor used by Albert Szent-Gyorgyi, we shall be concerned with the Creating Power that set up the structure that guides the function—the artist who made the recording which is our human existence and our experience of our total environment.

The last line on our proposed tombstone for the traditional

* Albert Szent-Gyorgyi, "The Drive in Living Matter to Perfect Itself," printed in the journal *Synthesis*, Vol. 1, No. 1, 1974. Words in brackets added here for clarification.

understanding of god was, "god is dead. Long live God." For the intelligent and thoughtful, life has departed from the traditional mental image of god. We are ready for an understanding of the divine that is consistent with scientific understanding of the universe and that leads toward a way of living that promotes peace in the heart, among people, and in the whole environment. We begin, then, with a kind of embodied knowing that I call "carnal knowledge."

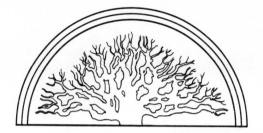

CARNAL KNOWLEDGE

A caricature is an intentional distortion that is made by exaggeration of salient features of the actual subject. Hence it is not without significance that the caricatures of Americans drawn by social commentators in other cultural groups picture us as expert mechanics but mechanical lovers. A flood of "How To . . ." books written by sex experts bears quiet testimony to our acknowledgement of feelings of such inadequacy. We tend to miss all the romance and delight of sexual relations and to convert making love into sexual engineering.

One reason for this unfortunate state of affairs is our traditional put-down of the human body. The official teaching for centuries has been that sexual intercourse is a regrettable and rather nasty necessity for the continuing reproduction of the species. It is an activity of the flesh, and as anyone who has read St. Paul's letters in the Bible knows, flesh is by its very nature sinful. He tells his readers that everything rotten in human behavior stems from the flesh, and his opinion has been treated as sacred revelation.

In former generations feelings of revulsion aroused by references to the flesh were mainly the result of religious conditioning. Modern television propaganda does little to improve our attitudes. Hucksters on the tube picture the body as a racecourse for competing pain-relievers; as suffering depression because of "irregularity"; as converting digestion into agony; as an arena in which saintly doctors battle against untimely, painful death; as giving off unpleasant odors that must continuously be suppressed by washes, sprays, powders, chemicals and perfumes; as a decaying, collapsing, stiffening, wrinkling, dripping, aching mass of misery. The only positive image of the human body presented by advertisers is found in the use of the female body as a sex symbol to capture male attention and in the use of young men and women in the prime of health to invite you to smoke tobacco so that you can forget lung cancer as you light up. So it is small wonder that few of us have much positive appreciation of the human body and that among us it is not customary to think of value in physical terms.

Consistent with such denigration of the flesh is the way in which we prize the high-level abstractions of pure intellect, i.e., intellect freed of any bias rising from inclinations of bodily existence. Having figuratively removed our head from our body we can calmly plan national policy in terms of how many millions of people in Russia we might kill in the first few minutes of a war as compared with our estimate of how many millions of our people the Russians might be able to kill. The figures we deal with are abstract quantities having to do with casualties rather than individual persons—mothers, fathers, children, babies. We have trained our intellect to act in such a way as to disconnect itself from bodily sensitivities—from the tears, the sickness, the churning gut, the physical revulsion against a nuclear holocaust of mass killing.

Such bodily revulsion is part of a way of knowing that is different from our common, and highly prized, left-brain, abstract, linear cognition. This other kind of knowing which has no need of logical analysis or verbal symbols is often called "intuitive." Modern research, following clues derived from a consistent pattern of impairments following upon lesions in one side or the other of the brain, has found that the powers of abstract intellect are localized in the left brain while the powers of intuitive knowing are localized in the right brain. We

Americans are mainly verbal, rational, that is left-brain, people. We do not highly value the knowing that comes without due process to the right half of the brain, the knowing of the artist rather than the engineer. We are simply irritated when someone knows something and yet cannot tell us how he knows.

Robert Ornstein of the Langley Porter Neuropsychiatric Institute in San Francisco writes that it seems probable to him that our emphasis on functions of the left hemisphere has dimmed our sensitivity to the true potential of right-hemisphere functions in somewhat the same way that the brilliance of sunlight makes the stars invisible. When the sun goes down we can see the stars. When we diminish our dependency on left hemisphere abstract intellect we have available to us more of holistic knowing that is centered in the right hemisphere.

My personal intuitive judgment is that intuitive knowing is more diffuse in its relation to the bodily modes of awareness than is intellectual knowing. To my way of thinking, intellect is chiefly rooted in what we see and hear, while intuition includes these two major senses but adds to them the complete sum of physical sensitivities. I also expect that the time will come when we will discover in the body receptive faculties for energy vibrations of the kind that would explain parapsychological phenomena. Carl Sagan thinks it probable that fully verbal, rational thinking is a relatively recent ability in human beings—perhaps only a few hundred thousand years old. Before that ability developed in the left hemisphere of the cortex, we relied on intuitive knowing and holistic sensitivity to the environment. We were, so to speak, alive in the wholeness of our bodily existence and all of it was an organ of knowing. So in these pages I shall speak of right-brain knowledge as "carnal knowledge," in order to emphasize that it is a knowing that involves the whole organic sensorium.

I am well aware that the term "carnal knowledge" has unpleasant legal meanings. To many of my readers the words will call to mind a feeling of nasty sexuality. Yet I have deliberately chosen to use the term because it will stand as a reminder that when I write about love and the knowing that comes through loving I am not following habits of thought most frequently found in popular piety. The love of which I write is neither a moral attitude supported by willpower nor a disembodied "spiritual" attachment. I'm concerned in these pages about flesh related to flesh, body related to body, the whole person in the totality of his or her existence in relation to the wholeness of the other. Such emphasis on the physical is necessary to offset the common tendency in church circles to speak about love as a general attitude of good will toward the other person.

Such a definition serves a very useful purpose for church people. Jesus of Nazareth said that the first commandment is to love God and the second is to love your neighbor as you love yourself. That first commandment is not difficult for modern religious people, since their knowledge of their god is a mental image derived from selected passages in the Bible. Such a mental image is easily modified to suit one's personal idea of what is lovable. But it is not always easy to love one's neighbor. He may disagree with your politics, frighten your children, kick your dog, and tell you to keep the hell off his property. So how do you love him? For that matter, how do you *make* yourself love anyone? You can pretend to the emotion, but you cannot force yourself actually to feel loving in obedience to a command.

A smart theologian thought up an answer to the problem of producing love on demand. He noticed that in the Greek language used by the original writers of the New Testament there are two words for love: *agape* (pronounced "ah-GAH-pay") and the more familiar *eros*. So this clever fellow said that *agape* is "Christian love"—the kind referred to when Jesus commands you to love your neighbor—and he said that this means only that a Christian must feel good will toward his neighbor. *Eros*, on the other hand, is "secular love." He said that *eros* means everything from a mild, friendly affection to all that nasty stuff having to do with sexual pleasure. So it turns out that Christians are ordered to practice *agape* toward their neighbors, but they don't have to feel the slightest trace of *eros* toward them. This means that you are faithfully practicing the command to "love" your neighbor so long as you do what you can to see that he is treated justly—even if you hate him with a purple passion. The popular expression of this solution to the problem of loving on command is, "You must love your neighbor, but you don't have to like him." Only people who think of the body as a chariot for carrying the head from place to place could be persuaded by such verbal sophistry.

Still, you will agree that it's clever. It gets you off the hook. No further need to be concerned about your puny capacity to feel positive affection toward others. Unfortunately, however, you pay a price. The verbal trick gives complacency at the cost of diminishing your possibility for real growth in your capacity to feel affection for others. I agree that it is a simple fact that very few people are able to love all of their neighbors. It is also obvious that one cannot love by a single act of will. But I am equally sure that any person can grow in their capacity to care if they have a genuine desire to do so, and nothing so stunts a person's emotional development as the helpless feeling that one has already achieved all that one can and all that anyone could reasonably expect. To say that "Christian love" is nothing other than good will is to give up on honest-to-God affection. As I see it, this is a way of gaining peace of mind at the price of surrendering a quality of character that is very close to the heart of religion.

In my dictionary, "liking" is only a less intense form of loving, and I think it sheer nonsense to say, "You must feel very intense affection for your neighbor, but you don't have to feel mild affection for him!" Yet this is a very popular religious way to talk about loving, so I feel that it is important to emphasize that this is not what I mean by the word "love."

The other popular way of talking about love in religious circles is to make of the relationship something "spiritual"— that is, disembodied or non-sexual. This is supposed to be far and away the best kind of loving. You could search through thousands of commentaries on the text of the two "great commandments" of Jesus without finding any slightest suggestion that the most powerful form of loving involves body as well as mind in total response to the beloved. Religious people apparently are not supposed to have bodies. They vanish from the neck down, or at least they pretend to do so for they have heard that when Adam and Eve lost their innocence they covered their genitals with fig leaves. The Puritan conviction that bodily pleasure is wicked was not constructed out of thin air.

Until very recent times, official church teaching held that even within marriage, sexual intercourse is permissible only for the purpose of begetting children. This is the voice of St. Paul reverberating down through the centuries. Paul makes it perfectly clear that in his opinion the best Christians are virgins. Hence in this way of thinking there is no place in proper Christian love for natural expressions of human sexuality. Provided that none of the residents had homosexual inclinations no slightest handicap would be placed upon it in a convent or a monastery. One could cogently argue that a person who grows up without the slightest inclination either to masturbate or to enter into any kind of sexual relationship with another person would, in St. Paul's view, have the basic potential necessary to being a natural-born saint. Need I add that most people today would consider such a person in some way sick or deformed and in need of help?

It is because religious people thus so commonly talk about love as either strenuous goodwill or non-sexual attachment that I choose to speak of the wisdom that comes through loving as "carnal knowledge." The love I speak of is not some kind of disembodied moral concern. I use the word in the way that we use it in common speech to indicate feelings of affection—the way that you love your parents, child, friend, lover, poodle, plants or home. Carnal knowledge is present in all these forms of love. It comes through as delight in being in the presence of the other. It involves speaking, touching, looking, listening, caressing, hugging, kissing and all other physical acts that are motivated by taking pleasure in the pleasure of the beloved. When you cuddle your child or your pet; when you hug your father or mother; when you visit a friend; when you provide water and sunlight for your plants; when you do things that make your home strong and beautiful; at all such times you are involved in bodily knowing or carnal knowledge.

The emotional center of carnal knowledge is the awareness that the self and the other are, in a very deep and real sense, one. In all genuine loving there is sensitivity to a basic unity that includes the diversity. It is there as a dim but motivating feeling in caring for house plants. It comes through in our relations with any of our household pets. We feel it most vividly as a single life shared by two different people when we experience mature, intense, delightfully sensual, affectionate and passionate love. *Eros*, in all of its forms, is central to the religious life because it is literally true that erotic love penetrates beyond the enchanted veil of isolation and makes us acquainted with the One who is hidden from the unloving. Carnal knowledge is knowledge of the Creating Power.

To understand how this is so let me remind you again that the ontological meaning of $e = mc^2$ is that this universe as a whole and in all of its parts is a single, limitless field of self-differentiating power that appears to our senses in some space/time locations as energy, and in other space/time locations as matter. As persons we are not made of some kind of ghostly, alien stuff that is different from all that is around us. Like all the rest, we are a complex set of vibrations within the total field, and this includes mind as well as organic structures. So personal life is intrinsic to the One infinite Creating Power, for we are persons and we are forms of activity of the One. Thus, we ourselves as well as the world in which we live are projections of a single living personal power in the same way that the world which you see on your TV screen is a projection of variant forms of a single vibrating field of broadcast energy. If we keep in mind that this is the nature of reality, then we can understand that there is no way that the One can be an object for you to observe—a something out there or over there for you to examine. The fact is that you are a limited variation of the activity of the Creating Power. The One is you, the knower, as well as all that you know, for there is no line of demarcation anywhere in the universe where the Creating Power ends and something else begins. There is no way that you can separate yourself from the ground of your own being and thus make it an object of knowledge.

However, this does not mean that the finite is forever excluded from awareness of the infinite. Knowing that the single Creating Power is the living inner reality of all forms of existence, we can understand that a feeling of unity between the self and any other person, place or thing is direct awareness of the One who is the creating and sustaining life of all. The knowledge that you and I share the same life as different forms of a single Self is most intense for those who have had the experience of being deeply in love with another person. As lovers have said in poetry and song through the ages, the knowing that comes through loving goes beyond words. As a finger pointing at a distant star calls attention toward it without touching it, so we try to describe the fullness of the experience of loving and our expressions flow in the direction of what we know but no symbols can touch our guiding light. It is not an intellectual knowing. It is as though the lover becomes his beloved. Throughout his whole body he is aware of a continuous longing that pulls him in the direction of the one he loves. The apparent borders of isolating individuality tend to fade away as the two separate lives become aware of unity in a larger life. The lover feels no precise and clearly defined interface where he ends and the one he loves begins.

Think back to your most intense experience of loving. Remember how your beloved pulsed in your blood, influenced your every decision, sang like a never-ending melody running through the symphony of all your interests. While you delighted in the differences between yourself and your beloved, you knew that these differences took place within a larger unity that is as real as your own body, as vital as your own heartbeat. It was altogether natural to think of your beloved as "heart of my heart," "life of my life," and "the other half of me." The myth of Plato which talks about love as coming home to the missing half of your own being is an apt expression of what you were feeling. All of our poetry and love songs are attempts to express this most treasured of all kinds of awareness: the carnal knowledge that "we two are one." And when the two are alone together the language of the body speaks more eloquently than words, as each finds delight in giving pleasure to the other.

Such in one of its most intense forms is carnal knowledge— the awareness of people that they are variant forms of a single life. Contemporary intellectual knowledge can, in theoretical understanding, grasp the unity of all existence. In carnal knowledge, the whole body confirms what the head understands: He who loves knows the One.

It is still, however, a limited knowing. A finite human being, except perhaps in the most intense forms of mystical awareness, cannot have direct experience of the endless reaches of the Creating Power. The lover's experience is like that of a man standing on a beach and looking out over the Atlantic Ocean. His limitations make it impossible for him to see the whole ocean. Yet there is no denying that the body of water lying within the field of his limited vision is in very truth the Atlantic. Similarly, the lover in his limited form cannot know the whole of the Infinite One. Yet, in his awareness that he is not a self-enclosed spark of life occupying a universe of alien stuff, in his capacity to feel unity between himself and the other in the experience of loving, the lover is in very truth aware of the One who is the single, living, continuous source of both the self and the other.

At this point in our thinking I feel the need to bring in a reminder both to answer the objections of some and to correct the intentions of others. I have been talking about carnal knowledge, embodied love. There will be some who say that they have had good sexual relationships without feeling the shared unity of which I speak. There will be others who take my meaning to be that anyone can have a great religious experience by going to bed with the nearest willing partner. My reminder is simply this: I am talking about love. I am not talking about recreational sex.

Not that there is anything wrong with recreational sex in itself. In recreational sex each person involved is primarily concerned with his own personal pleasure. Each relates to the other as a sex object rather than as a complete person, and the game is for each to use the other in ways that will help him gain for himself or herself a great orgasm. Depending on the circumstances and the partners, recreational sex can be a delightful experience. Some degree of it is part of the tentative beginnings of all true love relationships. Consciously or unconsciously a physical urging toward enjoyment of merging enters into the early stages of mutual attraction. Recreational sex is a natural desire—the necessary seed from which the beautiful flower of mature loving grows. This is another way of saying that self-satisfaction naturally precedes the capacity to find one's personal enjoyment in satisfying the needs of the other. Feeling good about one's own body, enjoying the pleasures it gives, is an essential part of that preliminary self-acceptance that is the necessary prelude to mature love for others. But the prelude is not the whole symphony. If growth does not take place and the relationship continues on a level where each of the partners is really enjoying only his or her sensations through the instrumentality of the other, then, however pleasant it may be, it is not love and it gives very little awareness that the two are one in the limitless life of the Creating Power.

Love leads a person so to identify with the feelings of the beloved that his happiness comes from giving her happiness, and she finds her happiness in his. Such joy in giving to the other does not exclude awareness of one's own feelings of pleasure. But these are, so to speak, a by-product rather than the central intention of the relationship. In mature love at its best, the feeling is not "you instead of me," but rather, "we together." The union is so strong that any pleasure is diminished unless it can be shared; any pain is more intense without the comfort and consolation of the beloved. The man who says, "I love you because you give me a thrill," hasn't yet begun to know what genuine love is. Whatever good there is in self-centered recreational sex, it is a stage of growth that contains in itself no deeply moving sensitivity to the One who is the real life of the two.

In my contemporary form of the ancient myth of creation I said that when the Creating Power particularizes himself in the roles of human beings he becomes in each of them not only a limited bodily form but also a limited conscious awareness. As a result of such limitations people generally do not know that they are, each of them, a variant form of the infinite One. The enchanted veil of limitation that surrounds each human consciousness thus becomes the source of all the suspense and excitement of the mighty drama of history.

From the limitless perspective of the One, the history of the universe is a most wonderful game. From the limited perspective of each human being, the same history is perceived as dead serious, final reality. Each of us knows that we have a date with death and there is no way to avoid the appointment. All that we have, all that we are, is tainted with incompleteness. To carry on while aware of the horizon around all our aspirations is to weave strands of futility into the red fabric of courage. Yet only thus can the game remain interesting. It is essential that the players on the stage of history generally do not gain absolutely persuasive knowledge that each of them is a role played by the Creating Power, for if the hero and the villain knew who they really are it would give the show away and they might fall laughing into each other's arms.

There is, however, an ever-present danger in human ignorance of the substantial unity that lies hidden in all variety. Man is the most dangerous of all animals. Hide from every person all sensitivity to the underlying unity and in the resulting competitive hostility the last man on earth might drown in the blood of his victims. The Creating Power, therefore, has to manage things in such a way that the tension of opposites will be taken seriously but not with absolute finality. Otherwise the drama, in its human form, would soon be over.

For this reason, using the terms of the intuitive myth of creation, we can be thankful that the One provides in each person the capacity to love and the longing for its fulfillment, as a cohesive bond between people. The desire to love and be loved is not the only important thing in our lives, but in most of us the urge to enter into such relationships is more continuously basic than anything else. We are bound together by our longing to be aware of union with one we love and who loves us. The single life of the individual exists in a continual state of hunger for completeness until that person finds some degree of awareness of the One who is the life of all.

Perhaps because our recent advances in technological expertise have vastly increased the power of our weapons and thus made us even more dangerous to one another, the Creating Power has in the past few decades greatly expanded the number of people who can understand the scientific theory that leads toward an intellectual understanding of the unity of all existence. Such understanding adds another cohesive bond among people, as some of these intellectuals are led on to consider the philosophical implications of their knowledge that the universe is throughout a single substance. Similarly the growing ecological concern of many who recognize human life as a variant activity of the total environment helps to diminish the hostility of competitive individualism.

There are, then, three different kinds of witness to the single reality that is the source and sustainer of all forms of existence: the experience of the mystic, the emotion of love, and the scientific understanding of the nature of the universe. Even so there is little danger that everyone will get the message and thus change the tension of opposites into a dance of celebration—at least not in any forseeable future. Such a transformation needs the motivation of more than news of a treasure hidden in the mystery of the obvious. Few have the intellect or interest to grasp the import of the change from Newton's clockwork image of the universe to Einstein's limitless, single, dynamic, self-differentiating field, that can appear as either energy or matter. Not everyone is capable of intense, deep, mature loving. Mystics with compelling vision are few and far between.

The news of the One in the many is abroad, but it is passed along as a wistful rumor that dulls the cutting edge of man's murderous inclinations without substituting the embrace of genuine affection. Only a creative minority is able to put all the evidence together and thus become capable of living fully the life that is paradoxically both limited and unlimited.

Yet I do not wish to imply that our human condition is one either of clear awareness of the Creating Power or of complete ignorance. People who are neither mystics, nor physicists, nor mature lovers may still have some feeling for the truth of the philosophy of the One and thus be stimulated to grow in sensitivity toward the Creating Power. Just as there are few real poets, but all who enjoy poetry have something of the poet in them, so there are few great lovers, but there is enough capacity in most people to care, to enable them to benefit from this new way in religion.

In any case, it should be clear by now that knowledge of God is not confined to popes and priests regardless of their claims. Neither is it the exclusive possession of evangelistic salesmen of salvation. The fact is that anyone who has ever said, "I love you," as an honest expression of deep feelings has in his possession the hidden key to the basic nature of the universe. And this remains true even if that person prefers to be known as an atheist rather than to be identified as one who believes in some petty and inadequate understanding of God. It also remains true for the lover who is unable clearly and precisely to verbalize what he experiences in his loving.

Carnal knowledge pours the blood of experience into the grey veins and arteries of theoretical understanding and brings abstractions to life. It is most intense in one-to-one personal relationships. But bodily awareness of the One who is both the self and the other includes a wide range of bonds of affection beyond the strictly personal. People love pets, wild animals, flowers, a city, a house, a washing machine, a piano, an automobile, a symphony or a novel. Indeed, the variety of possible objects of affection is unlimited.

You may have heard it said that "you should *love* people and *use* things." It is a valuable saying for it reminds us that it is wrong to manipulate other human beings for our own egocentric purposes. Yet this aphorism can be a threat to personal growth, for it fails to take into account the importance of loving material things, as I will point out in the next chapter.

LOVING THE WORLD AND THE FLESH

The New Testament contains a short moralistic homily that is generally representative of first-century, Hellenistic Judaism and is called the Letter of James. In that document there is a definition of "true religion" which gives expression to values and attitudes commonly found in our past. The author says that true religion is "to visit orphans and widows in their affliction, and to keep oneself unspotted from the world." These words call to my mind a picture of the world as a field full of dung and muck which the pure pilgrim must cross on his way to Heaven without getting any of the gunk smeared on his virginal white robes. Apparently most men died before their wives in the ancient world just as they do now, and since general life-expectancy was much shorter, this meant that most widows were left with small children. A religious man, then, was one who made a habit of visiting widows in their time of bereavement (with properly chaste and charitable intentions) and who showed proper, pious contempt for this world.

St. James and St. Paul differed in their opinion as to whether salvation is by faith or by works, by believing certain theological propositions or by doing good deeds, but they were of the same mind in their aversion to physical reality. James was disgusted by the world. Paul was disgusted by flesh. Both held as a basic part of their religion the opinion that there is something inherently filthy and corrupting about material existence. Material things, including human bodies, are at best obstacles and at worst a trap that prevents escape into the heavenly realm of pure spirit.

Their "holy contempt" for the world and the flesh had some odd and rather unpleasant results. Zealots who aspired to perfect holiness often refused to take baths or wear decent clothing lest they be thought to be too worldly. Many a pious person needed no words to remind others of his or her sanctity, since such a one moved in a distinctive personal atmosphere derived from a filthy body, which was accepted as one of the best advertisements of a pious spirit that properly mistreats the flesh.

Spiritual people, despite beautiful exceptions such as St. Francis, generally despised all animals as just so much animated flesh. Only people have souls that are imprisoned in their bodies. Animals have no souls. They were made for man's convenience and nourishment. Treating animals with the most revolting cruelty was perfectly acceptable among religious people. Similarly in the male-dominated social order of our past, women were repressed and exploited as part of religious other-worldliness, for the female body was seen to be a powerful temptation to indulge in the terrible sinfulness of enjoying pleasures of the flesh. Vows of poverty and chastity were natural expressions of earnest piety—chastity as an expression of avoidance of contamination by indulgence of the flesh, and poverty as an expression of avoidance of contamination by involvement with material things.

The properly pious other worldly person loved only spiritual things—and the list of such disembodied forms of existence wasn't very long: God, angels, the disembodied spirits of dead saints, the souls (not the flesh) of other people, and a collection of abstractly perfect entities that were believed to be the referents of such words as "beauty," "truth," "goodness," and the like. He felt compelled to avoid loving anything that could be seen, touched and tasted. Our auditory senses were thought to be less likely to involve us in getting spotted by the world, for sound seemed to be more spiritual. Music, for example, has no physical body that occupies space. It cannot be tasted, touched or seen, so it was held to be rather unworldly stuff. For similar reasons it was felt that the sense of smell was of more spiritual worth than the sense of touch, even though the odor of unwashed saints must have been difficult to bear. The use of incense in worship reflects not only the ancient belief that because spiritual beings have no physical bodies they feast on the sweet smell of roast lamb at a sacrifice, in the same way that the embodied priests feast on the cooked flesh, but also the effort to make the place of worship endurable to people with sensitive nostrils, when in the presence of so many who were practicing holy contempt for their own bodies.

In our new world of understanding, where the philosophy of Panentheism becomes the guide to wisdom, we reject other-worldliness. We know, by theoretical scientific knowledge, that the Creating Power is the inner reality of all that exists. In our feeling for the unity of all things through our capacity to love we know that the life that is in each one of us is equally the Life that is the source and shaping power of every form or body in the universe. In loving an automobile, a mountain, the restless ocean, a house, a rose or a postage stamp, we are loving the Self of the universe. Our knowledge of God as the ground of all being leads us to assert that the highest fulfillment of the human potential is found in loving the Creating Power in all that is around us as well as in ourselves.

And here I want to emphasize that this love for all things animate and inanimate is not unlike our love for other persons. Far less intense than the most mature, sensual and passionate relationship of a man and a woman, it is still a form of carnal knowledge—an awareness of the One in the unity felt between the self and the other.

When the object of one's affection is a household pet, love for the embodied other easily leads to recognition of mutual participation in a shared, larger Life. I cannot, for example, love my two pet poodles without becoming aware that the life that is in me is the same life that is in them. Their never-failing devotion shows that such sensitivity is mutual. The indefinable something that shines in their eyes speaks to the depths of my being. In those dark brown luminous orbs I feel the presence of all that is possible for conscious life. Lacking is only the capacity for expressing it in terms familiar to human beings. The limitations of the canine bodily instrument define the extent to which the One can come through. Only by such self-limitation within particular forms can the Creating Power become the familiar space/time universe. It is evident, however, to those whose eyes are made sensitive by loving that it is the same sun that shines through a small and not very translucent window as shines through a large and bright one.

As I have grown in my ability to care, I have found increased sensitivity to the presence of the Self of the Universe in all kinds of living things. I spend my summers in Nova Scotia. One of our neighbors there is a grouchy old seagull whose vocabulary is a combination of complaints and curses. At just about sunrise when the poodles and I go for our morning walk, we usually find him on an old piece of piling, bitching about the weather, the stupidity of younger gulls, the lack of decent food, or the overabundance of human beings. My daughter Penny has her Master's Degree in Speech Pathology and Audiology. With such an education I naturally assume that she is quite good at seagull talk. To me, at least, she sounds quite good when she tries to carry on a civil conversation with this dirty bird but he will have none of it. All he does is criticize her pronunciation and suggest that she fly off somewhere and drop dead. And his disdain goes beyond mere vocalization. Once he showed what he thought of Penny and me by flying overhead and dropping a large load that barely missed his target. Yet we both rather like the nasty old fellow. He is playing a particular role among gulls and he is playing it to the hilt. We feel that he would be terribly embarrassed if anyone discovered that under his filthy feathers there beat a loving heart.

Our relationship with porpoises that live in Mahone Bay has been more positive. One day a few years ago Penny and I were out on our sailboat when the wind died in a misty rain. We had an outboard motor that we could use to motor back to the yacht club from our position, which was several miles offshore. Seeing little prospect that the breeze would pick up again, I tried to start the motor. Nothing. Not a splutter. Something had to be wrong. I removed one of the spark plugs and found it fouled. I started to clean it, and as we were sitting quietly in the cockpit we heard, "Whoosh—Whoosh—Whoosh," the sound of air being expelled as in heavy breathing.

A family of porpoises had become curious about our boat and its occupants. There were a mother, father and youngster in the group. Round and round the boat they swam—close to and pushing above the surface of the mirror-still water. Their bright black eyes stared at us from a distance of no more than twenty-five to fifty feet. Three times the baby of the family broke from the circle and started swimming toward the boat to take a closer look. Three times one of the parents with a flash of speed intercepted the small one and butted him back to a safer distance. We couldn't hear their conversation, but my guess is that the baby was told in no uncertain terms that man is of all the beasts the most efficient killer. When that lesson had been learned and the appearance of the dangerous ones had been clearly impressed upon the mind of the young porpoise, the three of them took off, diving and surfacing in graceful play until they disappeared in the mist. For a few minutes life native to one element had greeted life native to another element and paused to examine and take the measure of the adversary. The feeling of kinship between ourselves and those denizens of the sea was very strong in both Penny and me. We felt them to be clearly variant forms of the one infinite Life.

Martin Buber, the great Jewish teacher and philosopher, speaks of having similar awareness of kinship with a tree. Many lesser writers have talked about how sensitive plants are to the emotional vibrations of human beings. My wife, for example, grows lovely roses because she gives them tender loving care. Once when she was a surgical patient in the hospital for a couple of weeks, it seemed that her major worry was her rose garden. I followed her instructions carefully. An observer would have seen me doing all the things that she would have done had she been in the garden. I even went out at least once each day to gaze on the bushes with approving eyes to show them how much I appreciated their gift of beautiful flowers. But you can't kid roses. They were well aware that I'm no green-thumb kid. They did produce blossoms, but poor stuff compared with their performance when Anne is around to love them.

More appropriate to my natural inclinations about plant life is my admiration for a certain tree on our Nova Scotia seacoast—a tree with its roots dug into rock—a tree scarred and twisted by its fight for survival against the tearing winds and ice of winter. To me this tree is a living example of courage, worthy of comparison with the bravest of men. Across the chasm of variant limitations that tree is a form of life that communicates with me as another form of the same life.

In Panentheism we recognize that the distinction between things that are "natural" and things that are "man-made" is a remnant of speech habits that reflect the old man-against-nature dualism. Knowing that people, like everything else that exists in the universe, are variant forms of the self-expression of the one, we consider "man-made" things to be as "natural" as anything else. The Self of the Universe acts through a bird to make a birdnest and through a person to build a house, and the one product is just as much a part of nature as the other. Thus we are not surprised that people have the capacity to love the manufactured products of human intellect and effort and to sense in such things a real feeling of kinship. When I am racing my sailboat and we are in close competition with another boat as we approach the finish line, I don't feel at all absurd as I pat her deck and say things like, "Come on, baby. Come on, old girl. Just a little more speed. You can do it."

If that sounds silly and sentimental because no amount of coaxing is going to make any difference in the performance of an inanimate object, let me remind you that a person with a problem can appear to be nothing but a "case" to the unloving, just as the unloving man can look upon any kind of material form as so much junk. But eyes that are luminous with love see a different world. The lover can delight in material objects and find some of his own reality in all that he can see, hear, taste, touch, or smell. When he does so he is in touch with reality, for the truth is that matter in all of its forms is a scintillating dance of the Self of the Universe in figures of vibrating energy and pirouettes of whirling power. Matter is altogether lovely and lovable for those who have eyes to see. More than that, it is a veil hiding the Self of our self; it is the gloves over the shaping hands that mold and support our very existence. Hence, the man who knows the One in the many rejoices in loving the world and the flesh.

Speaking of loving the flesh reminds me of the story about the man and woman who decided that they were compatible because both of them loved fish. After they were married they discovered that he loved guppies and she loved to eat fish dinners. It is one thing to love various animate forms of the single infinite Life. It is quite another thing to eat those forms. The fact that flesh lives upon flesh and life devours life is often cited by scientific impersonalists as support for their belief that the universe is nothing but a chance arrangement of mindless combinations of energy and matter. If the religious man is aware of himself as a particular differentiated form of a single universal life, and if this awareness comes to him through love for other forms of the limitless Creating Power, then how can he kill and devour that which he supposedly loves? And how can he love those other forms of life, all of which are involved in killing and eating? Even the plants in any woodland lot are trying to starve and smother one another in continuous competition for life-giving sunshine and water. Such observations are used to obliterate a popular "proof" for the existence of a God external to the universe he has made—in its simplest form the argument that the existence of a watch implies the existence of a watchmaker. Sensitive to the dark side of the process of evolution, the general tendency of modern biologists is to dismiss the existence of such a God, for they assert that no deity worthy of worship could have created and set in motion a process so necessarily involving continuous suffering and bloodshed. Their moral argument against a deity who is an immoral divine engineer, a distant spectator of the suffering for which he is responsible, is correct. There is no such God. But this does not mean that it is equally irrational to find the meaning of one's life in sensitivity to the panentheistic view of God as the Self of the Universe. We shall discuss our view of the nature of evil in later pages of this book. At this point I simply want to call your attention to a helpful way of thinking about the unhappy fact that life lives upon life as suggested to me by an experience reported by Loren Eiseley.

Once when traveling in desert country, that very perceptive paleontologist witnessed a fierce fight between a snake and a large desert bird. Near the scene of the conflict he found the cause of the struggle: a nest in which there were several large eggs. Eiseley said that the question at issue in that desert combat was whether the occupants of those eggshells would eventually wear the feathers of a bird or the scales of a snake. They would either hatch or be eaten, but in either case they would continue as variant forms of the animate continuum.

Life living on life is one of the countless modes of energy transformation in the continuously evolving flow of the self-expression of the One. In all of the limited forms of such divine self-expression life is always a birth/death process. Because I know that each particular embodiment is really another variant activity of the Self of the Universe, I know that life is neither lost nor gained in such transformations. A change of form is not a change of essential being. The Creating Power who is your inner constituent being, as he is of all other living forms, cannot be diminished by death which marks the dissolution of any one particular form of his activity.

In understanding this it helps to recall again the metaphor that reminds us that we are related to the Self of the Universe as a "fist" is related to a hand. Stop making a fist and the hand is still there. What appears to us as matter (more or less permanent stuff) is really a name for an activity that is going on at the time/space location where we perceive matter. Your bodily existence is an action, not a thing. You are an activity of the One, and in ultimate description you are the "hand" rather than the fist. You are the Creating Power, rather than an isolated ego temporarily imprisoned in a material body. You are an action of the whole universe and more, rather than some kind of temporary evanescent glow thrown off by an accidental biochemical structure called a human brain. And the truth about your ultimate reality is the truth about all embodiments of the single infinite life of the universe. As form they continually dissolve into one another, but the essential reality of the Self of the Universe, who is the Life of all life, remains constant in all change.

True, the process appears to our limited understanding as one that involves a vast amount of unnecessary pain and bloodshed. As we shall see in later pages of this book, there can be no good without the existence of evil. Suffering is the necessary dark side of pleasure. But I would also suggest that there may be less pain in the animal world than we imagine, since situations of extreme crisis anesthetize the nervous system. Most of us have had experiences of physical trauma in which we felt no suffering until some time after the excitement of the game or the accident in which we were hurt. An animal fighting for its life in the jungle may not really feel the agony we imagine as we watch the struggle.

In saying these things I have no wish to diminish sympathetic awareness of helpless suffering. Even if there is less of it than we imagine in the process of life living on life, we cannot be content while needless pain is felt by any life form—and our unhappy discontent is undoubtedly intended by the Creating Power as he incarnates himself in people. Such understanding and such sensitivities prevent those of us who follow the panentheist philosophy from casual killing since "after all it really doesn't matter." All that we hold to be good is derived from love, and love longs for the well-being of the other. We take the life of vegetable or animal only out of necessity for food to eat. Eating that which has been living is a reluctant necessity for those who love the world and the flesh. The tragedy of life devouring life is part of the pregnant dark that is the source of all the light we know. Our burden of regret is somewhat eased by the realization that the life we have taken was not annihilated by our action.

A large food company that sells materials for home baking once had an advertisement which said, "Nothin' spells lovin' like somethin' in the oven . . ." There is undeniable truth in that assertion. An important way of expressing love is to put something in the oven that has been prepared with loving hands. I would add, however, that such tender care should extend to all stages of the process of growing, marketing and preparing food for the table. Since we must live on other forms of life, the least we can do is to make life pleasant for the animals we will consume; to make their death painless and instantaneous; to honor the victim by the kind of cooking that transforms him into a truly delightful dish; and to serve him with a grace that delights the senses. Bad cooking is blasphemy against the Creating Power.

As sensitivity toward, and caring for, other forms of life in which the One is manifest are characteristic of the Panentheist who loves the world and the flesh, so also he will express his love by his sexual attitudes and activities. He will be joyously sexual in his loving, but his loving will be motivated by unity in which the two are known as variant forms of the one. His pleasure will be found in giving pleasure. He will not use someone else's body for his own private thrill and then try to excuse the deed by calling it "love."

Having said that, however, I want to go on and remind you that sex without mature love is not necessarily evil. Children will naturally be curious about sex, and in a healthy social order one should expect that there will be a common progression in sexual experience. After all, we do not expect a person to learn to play the piano without at first becoming acquainted with the keyboard. It is adult prudery about appearing in the nude that makes children play "doctor." When my three female grandchildren were aged nine down to five their young brother learned the manly art of standing by the potty to urinate. My daughter Polly tells of Willie's delight in his performance as the girls gathered round to watch. "In fact," she tells me, "when he first learned, he soon discovered how to release only a small amount each time so that he would be able to repeat the performance again in the near future!" If there is anything shameful in such an event it would be in the sanctimonious mind of some adult, not in the mind of my four emotionally healthy grandchildren.

As small children are not wicked in their interest in human sexuality, so also the sexual activities of teen-agers whose love involves a very large component of the biological urge to merge is not to be condemned. The harm that comes from the sexual activities of the young—unwanted pregnancies, venereal disease, fear of emotional rejection, feeling guilty or "dirty," etc.—is the result of ignorance. Unfortunately, the people most outraged by teen-aged sex are also the people who want to continue such ignorance. They oppose courses in sex-education in the schools on the ground that such teaching belongs in the home as part of the parental right to control children. "Right to control" in this case means the right to try to manipulate by fear of punishment in the hope that ignorance and guilt will prevent any premarital sexual activity. The opportunity to practice such motivation by anxiety apparently eases the fear and guilt in the parents who oppose adequate sex education in the schools, but it does so only at the cost of infecting the young with the same guilt and anxiety to pass on to the next generation. Only correct information, accompanied by opportunities for honest and open discussion with an understanding adult counselor, can lead to responsible personal decisions free from tendencies toward neurosis.

Good sex education includes a lot more than abstract lectures on the biological facts of reproduction. The opportunity to make wise choices in situations colored by very powerful emotional urgencies is dependent, among other things, upon knowing why you feel the way you do; how your feelings will probably change; what are the likely consequences of one choice rather than another; what attitudes and urges are natural to the male and to the female; what is the natural and normal range of sexual activities; how, in our culture, some activities can be "private" without being "dirty" or sinful; and what one may hope for in the mature consummation of sexual relationships. Such information takes us far beyond reproductive biology. In its positive attitude toward sexuality it diminishes fear and guilt and imparts a better chance for healthy human happiness. We cannot claim that good sex education will inhibit petting and intercourse among the

young, but there are honest grounds for doubt that the pro-
motion of ignorance and the practice of manipulation by guilt
and fear is in truth any more effective in such prevention.

We could agree that the demand for home-bred sexual ignorance among the young is none of the business of the
community at large were it not for the fact that the emotional
distortions of sexuality which have their source in repressive
households bring misery in compulsive behavior toward others. To give but one, rather extreme, example: I once counseled with a girl who had been brought up by parents who
instilled in her the ideal of "spiritual" love. She had been
taught to believe that any man who truly loves a girl will not
try to caress her body before marriage. The result was that in
her distorted way of seeing the world she felt that she had the
misfortune to date one "sex-maniac" after another. Because
she was an attractive girl the boys she went out with soon
expressed, by word or action, their desire to explore beyond
what her parents had defined as the proper limits. Finally she
found a real gentleman who showed proper respect and loved
her in proper spiritual fashion. After six months of dating he
wanted from her nothing more than occasional, not very passionate, kisses. So she married him.

After marriage she discovered that her husband continued
to "respect" her body. He showed little interest in sex. Soon
he began spending more evenings with various boyfriends
than with her. After long unhappiness she came to the difficult
realization that her husband was, in fact, a homosexual who
had married her to provide himself with a respectable cover
for his deviant interests and practices. Sympathy for the girl
caught in such a situation comes easily, but I also feel sorry for
the homosexual man who felt forced by our common con-
demnation of his peculiar sexual orientation to marry a
woman as part of playing a public role of normalcy. In addition I feel both pity and indignation toward the girl's parents
who "protected" their daughter with a lot of fantasy about

"spiritual" love and thus justified keeping her ignorant of the realities of sexual relationships.

To be against sexual ignorance, sexual repression, sexual censorship, and all other aspects of the nonsense that sex is, by its very nature as a bodily activity, wicked, is not to be in favor of completely unrestrained sex. As I will discuss further on in these pages, meaningful freedom is possible only within a framework of non-freedom. The reality of restraint makes choices meaningful and precious. The person who makes his or her body a public playground can't help but miss out on the special happiness that comes with giving the whole self to another as a deeply meaningful way of saying, "I love you."

The ideal, as I see it, is to be able to make such choices as an autonomous person—neither following a fashion of promiscuity nor a fashion of righteous abstinence. Each of us, in the light of informed understanding and with loving concern for all involved, ought to be able to decide for himself his own sexual activity in any particular set of circumstances. This is the ideal, even though it is probably true that most people have little capacity for autonomous decision making. Perhaps you will agree with me that one psychological aim of our social structures and customs should be to help people grow in that capacity. Such a goal will never be achieved by following the example of Dostoevski's Grand Inquisitor and feeding the common people pious falsehoods "for their own good."

Love for the world and the flesh does not make a person become a glutton or a sexual libertine. Neither does it impart a lust for money and property. The observable fact is that the misers and the big spenders of this world do not really love matter at all. They love money (which is an abstract symbol that can be exchanged for material things) and they love other symbols of status and privilege. The man who gloats over numbers in a bank book is not passionately fond of matter. His counterpart, the big spender, equally feels no devotion to things. He is a devotee of the cult of conspicuous consumption. He gets his pleasure by demonstrating to others what he can afford. He loves the feeling of egocentric power that comes from wild extravagance. Buying something you don't need, only to neglect and waste it, is not a demonstration of love for your property. The newly rich girl can show her status to others by buying the best of mink coats. She can make her wealth even more obvious by dragging it behind her over a dirty floor as she crosses the room.

The person who loves people in their wholeness, in what traditional language calls their "spirit" as well as in their body, has no need to impress others by the size of a bank account or contempt for expensive possessions. His pleasure comes more often in sharing rather than in accumulating. If money comes to such a person in abundance as a by-product of his work, he will find his increase of happiness in the ways that his wealth enables him to help others. It also seems probable to me that because his love is truly personal, and not an abstract feeling of good will, he will take the time and trouble to give personal help to other individuals. The rich who assist only tax-deductible charities and ignore the needs of friends and acquaintances seem to me to be lacking in loving sensitivity to the wants and wounds of people.

The person who loves the world will not feel guilty or ashamed of owning things that he honestly prices and actually can use. The monastic ideal of poverty, like that of chastity and obedience, has no place in a modern religious way of life except for those who are destined for a particular role in life that adds to the rich variety of human existence. Variety, including variety in things that people can afford to own and use, is not an unfortunate injustice that we should try to eliminate. Dull uniformity is contrary to the will of the Creating Power, as anyone can see who bothers to notice that in the evolving history of the universe the infinite One never does the same thing twice. So it is good that some men can afford a sixty-foot racing sailboat and others can afford only a ten-foot pram. Poverty is among the evils that all of us must work to eliminate, but not by eliminating economic variety and all that follows from it. The traditional Communist hope for a state in which human individuality is lost in the endless re-duplication of persons as functional social units adds to the variety of lifestyles among nations of the earth. We can be thankful, however, that such a homogenized social order will remain only a hope entertained by theoretical sociologists. Being contrary to the obvious will of the Self of the Universe that dream of uniformity will never become fully incarnate.

Love for the material world, as one aspect of our love for the Creating Power, necessarily involves genuine concern for the preservation of beautiful scenery; supporting efforts to handle waste material in ways that minimize pollution of the environment; fighting the wastefulness of planned obsolescence; opposing the manufacture of easily broken gadgets made of plastic ticky-tacky; appreciating things that are useful and giving them good care; being concerned about beauty as well as about utility in all of our possessions; and helping people to be involved in work of such intrinsic worth that they can take pride in what they do. To love the One in the many is to be a good ecologist who cares for all aspects of our earthly environment.

In thinking about our love for the world and the flesh I have often been led to touch briefly on the fact of evil. I think we are now ready to go into more depth and discuss the nature of evil as a necessary aspect of the One who is everything.

THE BITTER AND THE BETTER

When we are faced with hopeless situations in which nothing that we can do will gain the prize for which we long, then the ability to make sense out of life sometimes spells the difference between sanity and suicide. If one you love is taken by death; if a project that embodies years of labor and the sum of your highest hopes goes down in ruins; if you are helpless in the face of an incurable and agonizing illness; then it suddenly becomes very important to be able to place this darkness in the context of a larger light. Not that understanding will eliminate the pain, but at least you can be spared the anguish of the feeling that you are caught in the grinding gears of a mindless machine that neither knows of, nor cares for, your existence. Hence, it is good preventative medicine to develop a rational view of living that includes the shadows on the far side of brightness. Understanding the place of evil in a meaningful world is not just an abstract academic exercise.

Those of us who live in the new knowledge of our total environment have a special need for such a comprehensive philosophy of life. We have lost the traditional picture of the nature of reality that enabled our ancestors to trust in the goodness of life despite the reality of suffering. Without such a meaningful mental image we can no longer join them in affirming that "God is in his heaven, and all's right with the world." Instead we are left naked before the howling cold of creeping annihilation.

For many of us the biblical image of god as an ancient superman who lives above the sky and who is both all-powerful and all-good faded out of our way of interpreting the meaning of our existence precisely because we went through some agonizing sorrow or pain. We were told that God knows. We saw that he did nothing. So it was reasonable to doubt either the love or the ability of such a god. He doesn't care enough to help, or he wants to help but cannot. Add to such evidence of absence the tradition that this god is an invisible being who lives in outer space, and become aware of all the ways in which the biblical world-view is incompatible with modern understanding of the nature of things, and one comes to the realization that the biblical god was a resident of the world we left behind when we came over to the world of modern scientific and philosophical understanding. As a part of the only reality known to our predecessors this god was essential to their way of making sense out of life. Our reality is different and we are being forced to go beyond the past to ways of understanding that are consistent with contemporary knowledge of reality.

Religion that is centered around the concept of the Self of the Universe does not imagine the Creating Power to be the external spectator of our sorrows and suffering. The One is the single reality in all forms of existence, the one Life that animates all living bodies. Hence, just as all pleasant and happy experiences are his, so he is equally the sufferer of all pain, loss and tragedy.

Most people tend to have a mental block against the idea that our feelings could, at the same time and with the same degree of intensity, be equally the feelings of the Creating Power. This is because we have been trained by our culture to think of ourselves as totally isolated sparks of consciousness temporarily resident in alien flesh, and to think of God as an entirely separate being who dwells far distant from us in a place called Heaven.

Those who know the Self of the Universe, as a vivid part of their personal experience in loving and as a theoretical scientific description of the universe as a single dynamic field, reject both of those assumptions. It may help us to understand how an experience can be at once the experience of an individual self and the experience of the Self of the Universe if we remember the way that our feeling of self-identity pervades every part of our body. If, for example, I drop a brick on my toe, my whole body does not feel the pain. Only the member that has been injured suffers. Yet the pain is *my* pain because my toe is one with the energy system that I call my body.

Similarly, the Creating Power projects himself into pain-sensitive bodies. Each of these bodies is an infinitesmal differentiation of the whole Creating Power. My suffering is experienced by me as mine alone. Yet my suffering is also and equally experienced by the Self of the Universe as his. For the universe is, so to speak, his body, and suffering in any part of it is his.

Knowing this changes the shape of the problem of evil. The panentheist does not ask, "Why does God permit his creatures to suffer?" Instead, his question is, "Why does the Self of the Universe become the bodily forms of living things so shaped that they will experience suffering?" No longer do we wonder about the divine spectator "up there" who, perhaps, finds sadistic pleasure in watching his creatures squirm in agony; or who sits in helpless frustration, unable to help those whom he loves; or who may have left the theater during an intermission in the drama of history and forgotten to come back to see what was happening on earth. These were possibilities when the image of god was that of an external deity who has no part in our pain. Nor does it improve the situation to assert that this god once became incarnate and experienced human suffering on the cross. Having been through pain may increase his capacity for sympathy with those in agony, but it still doesn't explain why he lets such torture continue. The problem of evil has no satisfactory answer in terms of the old concept of god as a distinct and separate entity—a being totally other than man. It is one thing to be an uninvolved but sympathetic observer of pain, and it is quite another thing to decide to act in such a way as to experience pain in your own being.

Our answer to the problem of evil, then, will be found in giving rationally persuasive reasons why the Creating Power makes himself vulnerable to suffering by assuming the sensitive bodily forms of animal life in this space/time world. Particularly, why does he take on human forms that seem to be more vulnerable to pain than the other creatures? Other animals appear to suffer only in their now-moment of consciousness. They can feel painful memories and anticipation, but probably not to the same degree that we do (though this may be one of those human assumptions expressing our need to feel superior and our desire to minimize animal consciousness so that we need not feel any pangs of conscience about the way we treat such creatures). More than once have I seen the light of a whole life smothered in grief over the loss of one dearly loved. Equally often have I counseled with persons who had no joy in the present because they lived in an agony of dread of some event they expected in the distant future. Many a person in good present health is unable to live happily today when told that he must go to the hospital for surgery a month from now. Yesterday and tomorrow have long shadows among men. For their sake, I hope the other animals are not equally thus afflicted.

In thinking toward answers to the problem of why the Creating Power others himself in forms vulnerable to suffering, it helps to recognize that although we use few words to designate the dark side of life, the fact is that we meet many different kinds of evil in our common experience. I will deal with some of the major variations one at a time and try to see each of them in the light of the philosophy of panentheism.

I begin with the most pervasive and constant form of evil—

namely, the evil that arises out of the mutuality of opposites. What I am thinking of here is the fact that we become aware of good only because we are acquainted, either directly or indirectly, with evil. The happiness of victory is made real by our awareness of the pain of defeat. Health is precious because we are acquainted with illness. Success in any effort is pleasant to the degree that it was preceeded by a very real possibility of failure.

We do not prize that which has no opposite in human experience. For instance, people do not go around feeling pleased that the force of gravity is still active. You don't hear people saying, "Thank God for good old gravity! We've gotten through another day without falling off the earth." So far as we know, no one has ever fallen off the world to drift away in outer space. We have no slightest anticipation that anyone ever will. Hence no one lists the force of gravity as a highly prized value.

It becomes clear, then, that events and things are precious to us only when there are opposite events and things that we wish to avoid, and one soon comes to realize that this necessary mutual relativity of good and evil covers a very large part of the territory of human experience. It is pleasant to be a good cook because there are so many people who have not mastered the art. Any kind of achievement is sweeter if people generally know that many others have tried to do the same thing and failed. Just as there cannot be buyers without sellers, so there cannot be winners unless there are losers. Cops need robbers. Judges need criminals. Heroes need villains. Saints need sinners.

The mutual interdependence of good and evil becomes a more obvious necessity if you imagine a world in which every person is perfect in every aspect of his or her being: intelligence, health, beauty, personality, achievement, every possible human skill. Imagine, too, that these perfect people live in a perfect environment where there is absolutely nothing that could ever cause any kind of suffering—no problems to solve, no conflicts of any kind, no adventures into the unknown, no unexpected changes, no gamble or risk.

Sounds like Heaven, doesn't it? And, like Heaven as pictured in old fashioned piety, it would have another perfection added to all the rest: it would be perfectly boring. The Book of Revelation in the Bible contains passages in which Heaven is described as a place where saints, as if mounted on clockwork, forever and forever fall down on their knees and repeat automatic phrases in praise of the deity who basks in their adulation from his jeweled throne. From the perspective of our human limitations (and that is the only perspective we have), the prospect of spending eternity in such endless repetition would be deadly. Better to join the wicked in Hell where at least one might plot to air-condition the place. The truth that is in that jest is that we would choose a place of torment with the challenge to try to do something about it rather than choose the boredom of perfection.

It is not difficult for us thus to come to the realization that good and evil are, in fact, cooperating brothers, each of whom is necessary to the other. This basic aspect of our human experience provides the explanation of why, in becoming a universe, the Creating Power shaped himself into limited and imperfect forms in a world where pain and sorrow are inevitable. The Self of the Universe became the selves of people and of all other living forms in order that he might experience in all of these incarnations the joys and pleasures that are the opposites of the various forms of evil. It is a simple fact that without darkness there can be no light. We finite human beings would be totally unaware of light if it were always present, always of the same intensity. Contrast is necessary to awareness —for the One as well as for ourselves. So in us the Self of the Universe suffers in order that he may rejoice. He lives with evil so that he may celebrate the good. He is, I repeat, not the distant spectator of our pain, but rather one who feels whatever we feel, in the same way and with the same intensity. Just as pain in any of the cells of any part of our flesh is our pain, so our pain, as part of his limitless being, is his pain.

It is interesting to note that such purposeful acceptance of pain in order to create the opposite reality of pleasure is frequently characteristic of our activity as well as of the Self of the Universe. In many forms of recreation we deliberately lay ourselves open to real possibilities of unhappiness in order to increase our enjoyment. We know that the more difficult it is to win at one of our games the more pleasure we will derive from the victory. We could, for example, easily change the rules of baseball so that almost every batter could drive out a home run. Instead we see to it that such a feat is very difficult to accomplish. There is no joy in Mudville if mighty Casey strikes out, but on the other hand there would be no mighty Casey as a baseball hero if every fellow on the team could duplicate his skill at bat. We would rather take a chance on losing than lose the chance of significant winning.

Similarly in sailboat racing, when a fifty-footer is competing against a thirty-foot boat, we spend a lot of time, effort and money working out a handicap formula to give the smaller boat a time allowance that will make the race equal. And it is important to notice that the skipper of the big boat wants such equalization just as much as the skipper of the small one. It simply isn't any fun to enter a contest in which you have no chance of suffering defeat. If there are no natural obstacles to winning, we invent them and thus make it possible for us to lose rather than win.

In the same way we tend to seek natural challenges as tests of ability and endurance. The interest that people have in many types of research rises from the apparent insolubility of the problems they deal with. When the odds against success are very great the pursuit of the elusive goal is all the more rewarding. This is why men choose to try to make it to the top of Mount Everest, and when it has been done by one route another party will try to follow a different path that is said to be impossible. It is why a man will cross a wide ocean sailing alone in a very small boat. The sweet smell of success is brewed from the probability of having to endure the stink of total disaster. People will accept for themselves, and even take pains to create, genuine possibilities of all kinds of evil including a very real risk of being maimed, crippled or killed, simply in order to experience the pleasure and happiness that we experience only after having overcome real dangers. So it is quite understandable that when the Creating Power became, in one part of his limitless being, the mighty drama of the universe, he did so in such a way that there would be conflict and suffering in order that enduring the evil he might also experience the good that is made possible by the existence of such evil.

Another analogy from our human experience may help extend our grasp of the way in which the infinite One may identify with the suffering experienced by the finite person. Imagine a stage play in which the actor, John Smith, is playing the part of Hamlet. For the purpose of our metaphor let's say that John Smith so totally identifies himself with Hamlet that he forgets that he is John Smith. The Shakespearean lines feel to him like his own spontaneous speech. He experiences all of the stage scenes and situations as his real world. Thus, in that condition of self-forgetfulness, Hamlet's joys and sorrows, his triumphs and tragedies, are completely real to John Smith. For the time being he *is* Hamlet. When he faces death at the end of the play John Smith (as Hamlet) feels all of the genuine emotions that come to those who die under such circumstances in real life outside of the theater. Then the curtain goes down with "Hamlet" lying dead on the floor. The spell of self-forgetfulness and of total identification with the character in the play is broken. Hamlet is no more. John Smith gets to his feet, takes a bow to acknowledge the applause of the audience for a job well done, and then leaves the theater in company with his friends.

As with all analogies, this one is not perfect in all of its details, but it can serve to suggest the difference between role and reality. It shows how the Self of the Universe may project himself into all the variety of human roles in such a way as to forget himself in each of them and thus make possible for himself an endless variety of enchanted adventures. But when the curtain goes down, when each particular role is ended by death, the human, limited self that was that role awakens to knowing that it is really the Self of the Universe with memories of how well the role was played and with other parts to play in other possibilities of action.

As the actor knows the role he plays through and through but the role has no way of knowing the total life of the actor, so the Self of the Universe knows the many selves that he plays in the drama of history but these many selves have very little capacity to know their identity with that limitless Self. As part of the process by which he becomes a universe, the infinite one becomes limited focal centers of conscious existence. These focal centers appear to us in structures that we label as organisms. In each such organism the One is aware of all of the experience of that organism as a variation within his own boundless experience. Yet inside the limited consciousness of each bodily form there is a feeling of self-enclosed isolation. Thus the infinite One knows himself in each one of us, but in each of us the One is unaware of his infinity. The situation is similar to that of a person wearing those odd sunglasses that have one-way mirrors as lenses. On his side of the glass the Self of the Universe is completely aware of you or me, but on our side of the glass we see only the reflection of our own person.

This paradoxical not-knowing that takes place within knowing makes it possible for the One to produce the most mighty and wonderful drama imaginable. As the endless variety of sentient beings on earth (and undoubtedly on other planets in other solar systems) the Self of the Universe feels ravishing pleasures of mountained ecstasy as well as screaming agonies of the deepest-valleyed suffering and tragedy. He appears as the most wicked villain and as the most loving saint. Hitler, Stalin, or the mean guy who lives next door, all are roles played by the One. He is all of the killers as well as all of the victims. Each one of us is a character played by the divine actor in the vast drama of creation.

From our limited human viewpoint it sometimes seems as though the villains might finally triumph over the good people—the "good people" being, of course, you and me and all those who share our values and our way of life. And so they sometimes do in the short run, but not in any lasting way. For it is essential to the art of the dramatist to make sure that the good will somehow triumph in the end.

This does not mean that every play has to have a happy ending. When a drama takes place on the stage of one of our theaters, the final scene may well be one of tragic disaster. But it has to be *meaningful* disaster so that one becomes aware that all is not lost, and beyond the limits of the play the audience knows there is good that has not been annihilated in the tragedy. No one can be so poignantly aware of the sweetness of the distant trumpets of victory as is the defeated and dying soldier left behind on the field of conquest. His loss is tragic, but the trumpets still ring in our ears after the curtain goes down.

Similarly in the divine drama of our space/time existence, the evil is real, the conflict suspenseful, and happy endings are not the inevitable rule. But still, the evil is always subordinate to the good, and every darkness is pregnant with light. If this were not so, human history would long ago have dissolved into chaos.

He who knows the One in the many is able to accept this

interwoven dynamism of good and evil. He knows that the continuously contained conflict of opposites is a necessary part of the universal history and of his own history. He is not surprised to discover that every brightness has its dark side; that one man's victory is another man's defeat; and that every problem solved becomes in its very solution the source of other problems. Evil is always present to challenge the good, but the good is never totally and finally defeated by evil. As all solutions generate problems, so all evil generates goodness. Recognizing the necessity of this mutuality of opposites, the wise man comes to realize that asking for a world without evil is like asking for a world without space or a world without time. It is completely impossible to imagine a realm of finite existence without this mutual interdependence of form and background, light and shadow, value and disvalue.

Having accepted this truth, those who know the One through both intellectual and carnal knowledge do not measure the worth of their personal existence in terms of bringing about any completely satisfactory solution to the major problems they may confront in their lifetime. They do not expect to be able to bring into being any permanent good that will be totally free of any evil consequences. Contrary to the unrealistic optimism of muscular hopefuls who talk about "building the Kingdom of God on earth," the person who knows the Self of the Universe recognizes that a perfect society is impossible in the very nature of things. He practices, therefore, a wise and gentle skepticism which allows him to work to make things better without suffering from the illusion that he can make things perfect. His measure of personal worth is found in how he handles his conflicts rather than in whether he happened to win or lose.

Such teaching covers the far extremes of the normal curve of human behavior. In the necessary interplay of the bitter and the better there are some who appear to be born winners and there are others who appear to be born losers. The former may occasionally stir our envy but we seldom experience them as a philosophical problem that demands an explanation. It is the losers who trouble us, for if we intend to deal seriously with an attempt at rational understanding of the place of evil in the world, we must go beyond the position of those who can say, "Well, you win some and you lose some. That's life." There are many people whose small victories are as nothing compared with the immensity of their losses: the child born with an ugly hole in her face where her nose should have been; those who die young with painful and incurable diseases; helpless children brutally beaten by unloving parents; congenital idiots, outcasts, the hopeless and the completely unloved.

In such personal tragedies we still must affirm that the Self of the Universe is accepting the extremes of the role of suffering as necessary for the realization of the good. He feels all the physical and psychological agony of such people in his own being in the same way and to the same degree that they feel it. As a wound in your body is your pain so a trauma suffered in any embodiment of his being is his pain. The One endures the agony of the universe so that there may also be joy. These lost ones also call forth pity in other embodiments of his being and they are a continuous challenge to us to find ways of ending such suffering. As we have succeeded in ending the crippling power of polio and the extreme pain of mastoiditis, so we can hope to eliminate or minimize some of these personal forms of evil.

Meanwhile it is helpful to remember that these tragic roles played by the Self of the Universe are, like everything else, only temporary forms of his being. Death is not annihilation. It is simply release from a limited form—an awakening of the Creating Power to the infinity of his true being, which always was and always will be the true reality of every individual. In the One, nothing is lost. Possibilities locked in hopelessness in one embodiment can find fulfillment in another, and the greater the suffering of a person in this time/space existence, the greater the pleasure in the awakening on the far side of death.

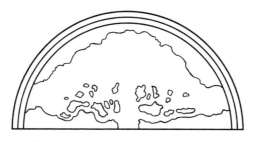

DECISIONS AND DESTINY

Most people are inconsistent in their attitude toward the way in which circumstances beyond their control shape their personal history. Events that were experienced as lucky accidents when they happened usually emerge in subsequent personal reporting as examples of how one may prosper by making wise choices based upon careful evaluation of the total situation. A capacity for happy forgetfulness enables us so to rewrite the narrative of our personal history that we can gaze upon the face of a hero in our mirror. Out of such forgetfulness covered by fantasy comes the boast of the "self-made man" who is quite unaware that he worships a very small creator. However, his behavior is only an extreme example of a tendency common to all of us. We consider ourselves to be masters of our fate when the train of events leads to moments of glory, and we thankfully lay the blame on misfortune when things go wrong.

If we had less need to prop up our sagging ego we might recognize that very few of our important choices work out the way that we thought that they would. Conditions beyond the reach of our personal possibility to influence or control very often produce unexpected consequences for good or for ill. Even when choosing our life work or the man or woman whom we will marry, the actual outcome seems to flow as much from chance as from choice.

Nonetheless, it is certainly true that our choices do play a part in creating our personal history, and it is evident that all of us place a very high value on our capacity to make meaningful choices. When I speak of "meaningful" choices, I refer to our ability to predict with a very high degree of probability the consequences that will follow if we do this rather than that. Such choices weave through the pattern of our days as one of the major factors involved in the unfolding of our personal biography. They impart a feeling of rationality to our existence. Without such meaningful choices our lives would be a nightmare of unpredictable results following upon free decisions.

Think, for example, what it would be like to drive an automobile in which the response of the machine to your movement of the controls changed in a purely random manner. At one time when you turn the steering wheel to the right the car turns left. At another time when you turn the wheel to the right the car continues straight ahead. When you step on the brake it may increase the speed of the car just as often as it slows the car down. Occasionally, when you touch the gas pedal lightly the car leaps ahead as if shot from a cannon. The next time, you may floor the pedal and instead of moving faster the car may come to a screeching halt. In such an unpredictable automobile you would still have freedom to decide what movements you would make in your attempts to control the movement of the car and you would have the bodily capacity to carry out your decisions. However, the unpredictability of the consequences of your choices makes your freedom to choose meaningless, and it seems probable that in such a situation you would soon be reduced to rigid, frightened immobility. Freedom to choose is meaningful only when the results of your decisions are in some degree predictable.

It follows, then, that the only worthwhile kind of freedom for any of us is dependent upon unfreedom, necessity, or rigid determinism. Predictability is a function of inevitability. That is a brief way of saying that a predictable series of events is one in which A is necessarily followed by B, and B is necessarily followed by C. It is only when A may be followed in random sequence by either B, C, D, or E, that the series is unpredictable. In the predictable series you can choose A knowing that it will result in B, so your choice is meaningful. In the random series you can choose A, but you have no way of knowing what you will get as a result, so your choice is meaningless. If we are to have freedom of meaningful choice there must be built into our space/time universe an element of non-freedom—a mechanical kind of unchanging inevitability. Such inevitability makes a large contribution toward our human experience of evil.

To go back to the analogy of the automobile—an engineer or a physicist could demonstrate that the dependability of the movement of the machine in response to the operator's touch on the controls is an illustration of what Sir Isaac Newton called "the laws of motion." These "laws" are brief general descriptions of relations between objects in space. These relations do not change within the common conditions of our human life on this planet. It is precisely because the laws of motion do not change that we can build an automobile and drive it safely. Yet it is those very same laws of motion with their rigid inevitability that will kill the driver if he tries to make a right-angle turn on a horizontal surface while moving at a speed of 150 miles per hour, or if he drives the car off a cliff, or if he slams it into a large mass of concrete. When such disasters happen, those who understand the mutuality of opposites as the necessary source of all values do not feel that the driver was being punished or picked on. They recognize that all of our freedom is grounded in unfreedom.

We cannot picture life that is worthwhile without the reality of meaningful choice. But if the Self of the Universe was to experience meaningful choice as a value, when he became a universe he had to include in the evolutionary process of continuous transformation an element of mechanical inevitability.

This mutual interdependence of freedom and necessity helps us to understand one of the very common forms of our experience of evil. It explains why bullets do not change their course and go around the heads of "good" people; why the law of gravity does not make an exception when a small baby falls out of a window; and why continuous eating of a harmful diet eventually will kill a person. If we value our freedom to make meaningful choices we will not complain of the iron necessity that is built into the creating process. To ask for a world without the real possibility of natural disasters is equally to ask for a world without the possibility of intelligent decision.

Thinking thus of our freedom to make meaningful choices calls again to my mind the behavior of those who play the role of villains in the drama of history. Granted that moral values are relative to the person making the judgement, and that one man's villain is another man's hero, the fact remains that few if any individuals have been greeted by universal affection in the human community. It is very probable that each and every one of us is somebody's enemy and each of us have some people whom we dislike. In a universe where all values and disvalues are mutually interdependent, conflict is inevitable. In the light of such necessity the panentheist who follows the philosophy of the One finds it possible to take attitudes of mercy, forgiveness and helpfulness toward his enemies.

In order to comprehend the genuine possibility of such attitudes we must begin with the realization that there is no such thing in this world as Truth, with a capital "T." In other words it is impossible for any human being to make a statement that will be true everywhere, for all people, at all times. Absolute truth is a highly prized illusion for all individuals who derive pleasant feelings of superiority from believing that they are among the happy few who share God's view of the universe. How sweet it is to believe that your way of seeing things and your particular understanding are free from all error! How nice to be able to assume that all who disagree with you are simply wrong!

The model for such faith in absolute Truth is simple arithmetic. Once you have learned that $2 + 2 = 4$, it seems that you have discovered a universal and timeless truth. You can't imagine $2 + 2$ equaling anything else at any time in history, in any other place, among any group of people. And given that elemental example of absolute Truth it is simple to go on and believe in all kinds of absolutes.

Unfortunately, however, the feeling of inevitability about arithmetical "truth" is due to nothing more than the way in which numbers are defined. When you were learning arithmetic you learned that $2 = 1 + 1$. You also learned that $4 = 1 + 1 + 1 + 1$. Therefore, instead of being an eternal truth straight out of the mind of God, the statement that $2 + 2 = 4$ is merely a shorter way of making the tautological statement that $1 + 1 + 1 + 1 = 1 + 1 + 1 + 1$. Thus the "absolute Truth" of the statement turns out to be nothing more than an awareness of identity rising out of exact repetition of the same meaning in two different sets of symbols. It is like saying "A is A"—an assertion that tells you something about how people in our culture use abstract symbols, but one that gives no information about the real world in which we live. When you look at the actual, non-symbolic world around you, you will discover that although simple arithmetic is a useful tool, it doesn't give much more than an approximate correspondence with actual items in our environment. While dealing only with words inside your head, one apple plus one apple equals two apples. If, however, one of the apples on the fruitstand in the market is rotten, the housewife who is buying them doesn't think that in this case one apple plus one apple equals two apples. As a matter of fact, no two anything anywhere in the world are exactly equivalent if we examine their structure with powerful instrumentation. Furthermore, when dealing with things rather than symbols, we come upon such oddities as the fact that although one gallon plus one gallon equal two gallons in mental arithmetic, if you pour one gallon of water into a container and then add to it one gallon of pure alcohol, the result will be less than two gallons of liquid.

Even in terms of adding abstract mental symbols, there are various conventional systems that demonstrate that our way of defining and using numbers is an arbitrary cultural invention. All of us know a kind of arithmetic, for example, in which $10 + 4 = 2$ rather than 14. If it is ten in the morning and I tell you that I will meet you in four hours, at what time will you expect to meet me? So in arithmetic, as in anything else, there is no such thing as Truth with a capital "T." All of our knowledge is more or less probable; true in some circumstances and false in others; lacking in completeness; an approximation rather than a duplication; a map rather than the territory.

Only in religious dogma does any intelligent and educated modern person pretend to possess absolute Truth, and dogma is a special kind of language used in theological games which, however interesting they may be to the players, have little more relevance to life than the intricacies of a game of chess. Like it or not, we live in a world of numberless small truths that are more or less valid. No human mind has the capacity to describe anything as it "really" is in the mind of the Self of the Universe. Knowledge is relative rather than absolute; pluralistic rather than simple. This statement includes all that I have to say in the pages of this book, all that I can tell you about the philosophy of Panentheism. Confident as I am of the importance and relevance of what I am writing, I recognize that confidence as having its source in my particular, personal history and in all that characterizes me as a person. I share this teaching with others in the faith that there are other people like me who will find my viewpoint making their own experience of the world more luminous. Like me, they will be people who can live with open-ended questions—people for whom dead certainty is certainly dead. They will be people who recognize that although we cannot have perfect knowledge of reality, a reasoned probability that is consistent with the general level of contemporary knowledge is much to be preferred over the rigidities of past authoritarian pronouncements or the accidental conclusions of unfounded guessing.

When we turn from intellectual assertions about the world to value judgements, the limitations of our capacity to know become even more evident. What seems terribly wrong to one person appears to be not nearly so bad to another. Our values are absorbed from the cultural group in which we live and modified by our personal thought and experience. I favor legal freedom for a woman to decide, with the advice and counsel of her doctor, whether to terminate a pregnancy by abortion or not. I am well aware that many people consider abortion under any circumstances to be extremely immoral. I can justify my position. They can justify theirs. The opposing value judgments are culturally conditioned, though, unfortunately, neither party to such differences of opinion is often aware of the fact.

One criminal may know that what he calls "the establishment" disapproves of his conduct to the point of making it illegal, but because he feels that he is an outsider it is his honest judgment that he owes no obligation to those who make up such rules. Another criminal may be able to identify with the establishment, but justifies his illegal behavior by claiming the guidance of a higher loyalty. During the Nixon Administration several men in high government positions were convicted of various crimes, but showed no feeling that they were guilty of wrongdoing, because they were convinced that their primary obligation was to reelect and protect the President. If we are honest with our assessment of how we might feel in their circumstances, most of us will find it not improbable that these men felt rather heroic and noble in the risks they took to fulfill what they deemed to be their moral duty. From their subjective viewpoint the tragic thing was not what they did but rather the fact that they were caught.

As there is no such thing as absolute Truth, there is no such thing as absolute "right" and "wrong." The villain, even as you and I, does what he feels he has to do in terms of his subjective view of the world and of his awareness of the choices open to him. The law, insofar as it represents a wide consensus of public opinion within a particular cultural group, has a right to condemn the criminal, but the criminal also has the right to consider himself a victim of the law. Neither value judgment can legitimately claim the endorsement of the Creating Power. On the contrary, the differences of opinion as to what is right conduct and what is wrong have their source in his intent, so far as we can infer the divine will from observation of the creating process.

The Austrian psychiatrist, Viktor Frankel, called attention to this when he wrote about the variations of individual destiny among people. By "destiny" he meant all of those aspects of our existence that we did not choose and cannot change. To give only a very incomplete list of such given factors in individual life, we did not choose the time and place of our birth; our parents with their peculiar individuality and their social and economic status; our male or female sexuality; our bodily comformation and its relative state of good looks and health; our inborn talents and aptitudes; and all through the days of our years the countless circumstances beyond our control that opened or closed doors of opportunity.

It is not difficult to imagine what a great difference it makes in life to be born the son of well-educated, very wealthy parents in Boston, Massachusetts, rather than to be the son of a starving prostitute of the Untouchable Class in Calcutta, India. The powerful athlete was given something that was omitted in the ninety-pound weakling. Truly great singers are born rather than made. There are very narrow limits within which education can improve the minds of the congenitally stupid.

Fortunate circumstances beyond personal control are the basic ingredients in most success stories.

When we are aware of the vast differences made in our lives by the given circumstances of our becoming what we are, we will tend to be more tolerant of other people. What Frankel calls "destiny" could equally be called the assignment of particular roles in the mighty drama of history. The One has so arranged it that there will be differences among human beings, including moral differences. Thus the cast of characters is well-supplied with villains as well as with heroes; with those who love as well as with those who hate. If you go deeply into the total personal life of the worst criminal, you will find yourself experiencing a kind of sympathetic understanding of his deed, even though you do not condone the crime. Such, I believe, is the attitude of those who understand the universe as the self-expression of an infinite, personal Creating Power.

In saying this, I do not intend to imply that human beings are nothing but puppets, with the Self of the Universe pulling the strings. I simply wish to point out that the choices open to each one of us vary according to the unique history and situation of the individual. Persons are to some degree responsible for what they do, but they are far less responsible than they would be if they were exact duplicates of one another, and the choices open to them were identical for everyone.

The conditions of birth and the subsequent history of some individuals make it almost inevitable that they will lead lives that others judge as evil. *Almost* inevitable, but not quite. So it seems to me that others may judge them as in some degree responsible for their own choices. The facts of personal destiny ought to help us to temper such judgment with compassion. While protecting the community from the harmful activities of the criminal, we should also feel an obligation to understand his conduct and to do what we can to assist him toward a more acceptable way of living. Vengeful punishment will be forbidden to the Panentheist.

Variations in destiny place one man on the judicial bench and the other in custody waiting to be sentenced. The judge who is aware of the necessity of such variant roles in the drama of history will do his duty, but without lust for making the criminal suffer, without self-righteous feelings of superiority. If the judge is aware of the ways of the Creating Power in assigning roles to people, he may have the grace to remember that without that poor bastard standing before him, and countless others like him, the judge would be out of a job.

Value judgments are both subjective and relative, and they are conditioned by personal destiny, thus making possible the continuously contained conflict that gives interest, excitement and adventure to the ongoing drama of history. Within that drama there is also an element of rigid necessity that makes meaningful decisions possible. As we have seen, both the necessity and the variations in destiny often become the source of pain and heartbreak. Yet we have also seen that because of the values they make possible, we would not want to live in a world without them.

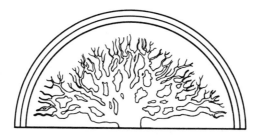

DELIGHTFUL DEVILTRY

A wise old friend with a twinkle in his eye once told me that he felt it was very important to resist temptation, provided that one was not pigheaded about it. "I always make one good try at it," he said, "and then, after that, I recall the practical good sense of the aphorism which says, 'If at first you don't succeed, give up.'"

He made it sound as though giving up was easy, but there are some forms of temptation in which one truly feels so torn by conflicting desires that a decision to do one thing or the other makes a person feel miserable. Since our experience of evil includes all situations that we find repellent, this inward feeling of a division in personality—such that we want one thing while at the same time we want its opposite, and the situation is such that we cannot have both—is a common part of the dark side of existence. When this conflict involves standards of personal behavior, we have been taught to label the "good" desire as the voice of conscience. As Sigmund Freud pointed out, the "good" desires are easily distinguished from the others because they carry a feeling of having emanated from some voice of authority. Someone in your past is telling you what you *ought* to do or what you *should* do.

As a boy I was told that my conscience is "the voice of God." The same people told me that babies are brought by the stork. Other boys in my neighborhood straightened me out about the facts of reproduction, but it was many years before I came to understand that "conscience" is simply a name for an individualistic, subjective value system imparted by social conditioning when a person is young. The agreement in a social group that certain kinds of behavior are approved and other kinds are disapproved is the consequence of a shared cultural environment rather than shared sensitivity to universal commands of the deity.

In our culture there is general agreement that it is wrong to commit murder. Anyone who did so would probably suffer some pangs of conscience. He or she would feel guilty for having done something wrong. But imagine a robber band that preys on lone travelers along some desolate stretch of wilderness road. Suppose that the band provides for its own safety by a very strict law that all agree upon and that is drilled into all the children born to members of the band. The law says that you must always kill any person you rob and you must always dispose of the body so that there will never be a witness to testify against the band in court. So a child is brought up among the outlaws and he learns by word and example the great importance of the code they follow. One day, however, he takes pity on a helpless old lady after robbing her. Because she reminds him very much of his own mother he does not kill her. It is altogether probable that such a young man would suffer from a bad conscience after the event because he did not commit murder! The voice of God? Nonsense!

A voice of conscience that thus contradicts our norms of moral behavior reminds me of a recording that I once heard. It was made by two British comedians as a dialogue between a boy and his father in a tribe of cannibals. The boy had suddenly decided that it is wrong to eat human flesh. His announcement had shocked all his family and his father had the task of persuading the lad away from such shameful deviant behavior. The father proceeded to use all the familiar arguments that we use to persuade conformity to any moral practice: What will the neighbors think? Your crazy ideas are making your mother sick. Your ancestors have always eaten people. Your father eats people. You will be sick and puny if you don't get good solid nourishment by eating people. Look at the Medicine Man—admired and feared by everyone, and he eats people. You won't have a chance to become chief of the tribe if you don't eat people. "If the Great Spirit hadn't intended you to eat people he wouldn't have made them out of meat!" But the argument that finally changed the boy's mind was the assertion that if you are going to say that it is wrong to *eat* people, then the next thing you will say is that it is wrong to *kill* people—and that is an obvious absurdity.

I might adapt that final form of persuasion to our present discussion. The argument would run as follows: If you are going to say that any inner feeling of being pushed toward a line of action that someone in your past labeled as "good" is the "voice of God speaking through your conscience," then the next thing you are going to say is that good behavior is always a matter of conformity to past authority, and that in the past all authorities had infallible knowledge of the will of God—and obviously such assertions are absurd.

Unfortunately, abandonment of traditional ways of talking about the problems of ambivalent will does not eliminate the difficulty. People who have given up old-fashioned piety will often describe their inner conflict as a struggle between the good "I" and the wicked "me." "I" tries to make "me" do some unpleasant task, or give up smoking, or stay on a diet, or be more tolerant. "I" is always the good guy. He represents our ideals, the perfect person that we once were told that we ought to be. "Me," on the other hand, is a wicked, lazy, self-indulgent rascal who time and again leads the good "I" astray. The tug of war between these two sides of the same person can add interest to living, provided that "I" has a good sense of humor so that he doesn't take himself very seriously and he can be amused by "me." But very often that is not the case. The good "I" in a vast number of people was created by the demands of some adult, or group of adults, who wanted to force a small child to grow up as an angel rather than as a human being. The defenseless small one was conditioned by rewards and punishment to strive for perfection. As an adult, this same person continues to hear the incessant demand for superhuman perfection. The good "I" shines on the far edges of fantasy as the unreachable star that must be reached. The bad "me" comes to be experienced as the shameful and loathsome creature I am because I do not become what I ought to be. "I" hates "me"—the publicly known person. Such hatred can even motivate murder. Many a case of suicide is a form of murder in which the superhuman ideal "I" is provoked to such anger by the all-too-human "me" that he kills him.

Such disastrous results of having been conditioned to demand perfection of oneself are common enough, but even more frequent is the occurrence of interpersonal hostility generated by perfectionism. "Me" represents the imperfect, human side of the self, the aspect of the self that is similar to the human attitudes and behavior of all other ordinary human beings. Since the angelic "I" hates the earthy "me" in my own person, it is natural to extend that same angry rejection toward others who behave like "me." That which a person hates in himself, he will hate in other people.

There is also another unhappy consequence of this inner demand for perfection. We have already noticed that the Self of the Universe others himself in us in such a way as to place a veil of unknowing between the finite role that he plays in us and the infinite unity of his reality as the ground of all being. We said that he also gave us the need and the capacity to love and be loved so that we could have some awareness of his single life in all living things, his constituting activity in all forms of existence. Without exercising that capacity for loving we are incomplete human beings, trapped in small cages of ego. Without being loved by others we are isolated from well-springs of happiness. In some degree the perfectionist is cut off from such relationships that satisfy the hunger of the heart. Believing that he can only be acceptable to others if he lives as the good "I," the perfectionist will very often learn to become a good actor. Although he cannot force himself to feel loving toward despicable ordinary humanity that behaves as his "me" wants to behave, he can behave in such ways as to pretend to be loving. He can offer the friendly handshake, say the right words, arrange his face in an approving smile. He can follow the directions of books that tell him how to win friends. He can make a sensitive response to the wants and wounds of others even though the motivation has its source in his head rather than in his heart. In short, he can become an expert at playing the part of the lover of mankind.

Such a game of make-believe loving serves many useful purposes, but there is always a dark place of anxiety and sorrow at the heart of it. For the sad thing is that the perfectionist knows that he is playing a game of pretense. As a result he must always keep a barbed-wire barrier around the vital center of his person lest those who penetrate too far in intimacy discover that he is empty in the middle of his being. He cannot believe that any other person could truly care for him if they knew more about him than the public image he so carefully projects. Furthermore, when people do respond to him with all the signs of genuine affection, the perfectionist can find no deep and durable satisfaction, no assuaging of the hunger of his heart, for he must think of their caring as directed toward the role he plays rather than toward his genuine self—the rotten "me" that he conceives himself to be.

An approach to healing the tragic inner conflict of the ideal person and the actual person can be made by the realization that in the individual person, as well as in the total environment, the Creating Power brings about the experience of "good" in all of its forms by dynamic interaction with all the various forms of "evil." It is impossible to have the one without the other, just as it is impossible to perceive a figure without a contrasting background.

If someone should ask you to take a totally black piece of paper and draw on it a picture of a totally black dog swimming in a totally black sea of ink on a night so dark that there is not the faintest suggestion of light, obviously it couldn't be done. But notice that I can talk about such a picture, even if it is impossible to draw it. This is because we make distinctions in words that are impossible to make in our actual experience of our space/time environment.

For instance, we can talk as if the world were a chance collection of independent items, even though in actual experience all forms of existence are mutually interdependent as differentiations of a single continuum. We are aware of the One in the concepts of theoretical science, in mystical experience, and in the union felt in loving. We know that all existence is a single system of variant activities through our study of ecology. The whole creates and sustains the parts and the parts are variant forms of the whole. Frogs do not exist without ponds. Ponds do not exist without valleys. Valleys do not exist without geological history. Geology is part of the flow of transformation in a planet that is derived from a star—and on and on to the far edge of theoretical knowing. Yet despite the omnipresent One, our senses tend to tell us of a world that is a collection rather than a continuum, a many rather than a one. A very large part of the reason for this is the limitation of our senses, which can perceive either form or background but are unable to be simultaneously and equally sensitive to both as a single reality.

A simple illustration of this truth is shown in the following well-known picture. Is it a picture of a single white vase, or is it a silhouette of two faces about to kiss? Notice that you can see *either* the two faces *or* the vase. It is impossible to be equally vividly aware of both at the same time.

This face-or-vase picture shows that our perception is inevitably selective, and this is why we tend to experience the universe as a collection of items even though it is actually a single, seamless ocean of flowing forms in continuous process of transformation. We can talk about "good" apart from "evil," we can easily think of the two as separate entities, in the same way that we can see the white vase apart from the two black faces. But reality is not "good" plus "evil." In actual fact the outline of the one is identical with the inline of the other. Reality is good/evil in the same way that it is one/many, freedom/necessity, pleasure/pain, love/hate, or life/death. All of the various instances of dualism are apparent rather than real. The Self of the Universe produces the drama of creation through the tensions of opposing currents within a single whole that is a subordinate field within his own being.

So your temptations are not due to the voice of God resisting the enticements of the Devil. Such symbolism once represented the best that people could do with explanations. Now that we can do better we must speak of the old symbolism, which could be counted true for our ancestors, as pious super- stition. Neither is the conflict of inner desires due to some kind of split personality. In the single integrity of your per- sonal existence there is a necessary dark side as there is in all the world. It is the rich dark earth out of which grows what- ever virtue you may have. As the small comic strip character named Pogo once remarked with all the wisdom that is found among the childlike, "We have met the enemy, and he is us!"

When you know that the "enemy" is an aspect of your own reality and indispensable to all your feelings of worth, you have a chance to develop that most wonderful of all virtues: a gentle cynicism that is the necessary atmosphere of an inclu- sive capacity to care for people.

Being aware of your own failings as a natural part of your own humanity, you become able to accept the failings of oth- ers and to like them just as they are, warts and all. You know that your own public reputation for virtue goes far beyond the reality, and this frees you from the illusion that others are not worthy of your affection. None are so unloving and judg- mental as the righteous who angrily disown in themselves the tendencies they observe in others. The gentle cynic knows that given the same situation that the other person is in, and given that person's individually unique past history, he would un- doubtedly do whatever that other fellow has done. Being gently skeptical of any virtue he may have, he can forgive the other fellow's vice.

Indeed, when one comes thoroughly to understand the unity of wickedness/virtue one can accept and often be thank- ful for immoral urges as the source of one's virtues. For example, a man who in a fit of anger has done something that he deeply regrets will have more than ordinary capacity to understand other people who lose their temper. Or think of the sourly prim maiden lady who wears her virginity as a badge of honor, if not as a divinely bestowed halo. She finds it easy to look with contempt upon the scandalous behavior of other women until she herself has a love affair. She may not immediately blossom into a sweetly tolerant disposition but the experience will, I am convinced, change her attitude for the better.

Again I must caution you lest you misunderstand my counsel. I am not advising you to suppress your own moral ideals and go out on an orgy of wickedness so that you can be more tolerant and affectionate toward ordinary fallible people among whom you live. Artificial immorality is as hypocritical as is artificial virtue. Flaunting your flaws is as unreal as pretending to have none.

Those who know themselves to be living as a form of the Self of the Universe in the drama of creation seem to find it easier to live in terms of their own complete reality rather than in terms of hidden vice and pretended virtue. The trick is to be able to accept all that you are as your role in life, basically defined for you by the Creating Power in the conditions of your destiny. Knowing the necessity and the positive contribution of the dark side of your self should make it easier to make peace with your internal enemy. When you follow the philosophy of Panentheism you do not expect all-around perfection in yourself or in anyone else. You are aware of your own innate rascality, and you are not surprised to find evidence of the same in other people. When your unacceptable urges sometimes get expressed in action, you do not hate yourself or call yourself bad names or mope around feeling guilty. If others were hurt by your deed and you can make amends without causing a bad situation to become worse, you do so. Otherwise you go on a wiser person with enlarged sympathetic understanding for others who occasionally deviate from public norms of proper behavior.

The importance of thus accepting yourself as a saintly devil or a devilish saint comes out in our most intimate friendships. When you are with a person whom you trust completely in the security of mutual love, one part of your happiness is the blessed relief of simply being yourself, your whole self, without anxiety about the impression you may leave with your friend. No longer do you have to go through the labor of carefully weighing words and making conversation. You can simply let communication flow so easily and spontaneously that you hardly know what you think until you hear what you say. You reveal thoughts and feelings just as they are, without any moralistic "should" or "ought." How good and pleasant it is thus to have your whole self accepted, the dark side as well as the bright, by a well-loved person who has no inclination to judge you! Even better is the ability thus to accept oneself, the whole range of one's being with good-humored tolerance.

When two people are gathered in loving trust they sometimes enjoy revealing to each other the devilish side of their character—not in a mood of guilty confession, but rather in delight at mutual discovery and acceptance. It is fun to discover that your own most wicked thoughts and unfulfilled urges are not private peculiarities but are present equally in the one for whom you care. Our ability to love and to forgive is largely dependent upon such discovery that we all share the same human nature. We could all live more tolerantly with those around us were it not for egocentric fear which causes us to hide our human limitations from our neighbors.

Do people find it easy to talk to you about their moral lapses and unacceptable urges? If they do it is a fairly reliable sign that you have made friends between your "I" and your "me." Having given up the tragic foolishness of "hating yourself in the morning," and feeling guilty about your own humanity, your "I" no longer judges your "me." This non-judgmental quality of your person will shine through your approach to others, and they will respond in blessed relief at being able to relax in spontaneous selfhood while they are with you.

Temptation, then, is not an evil in itself. It is the stuff you grow on—the inner dynamic tension that creates and sustains your values. It is good to be aware of a wide variety of wants that may not be either socially acceptable or personally realizable, but which nonetheless you accept as a subordinate aspect of your own personality. If you try to suppress those that conflict with your ideals, you will be trying to get rid of part of your own being. It is truly possible to acknowledge as your own the dark side of your personality without acting on the urges and impulses that are there. Such acceptance of your whole self will make you a more humane and loving person. As you become more loving you become more sensitively involved with reality and thus more aware of your true relationship with the Self of the Universe.

TOO LITTLE TIME

Somewhere, years ago, I saw an allegorical image of time. It was a picture of the face of an enormous clock on which stood two human beings, one a mere child and the other very old. Both had their hands on the minute hand of the clock. The child was trying to push the clock ahead to make time go faster. The old person was trying to hold the clock back to make time go more slowly. These contrasting attitudes toward temporal transformation remind me that all of us stand between memory and anticipation, and either one can be a source of happiness or of sorrow.

On the whole it seems easier to think of the flow of change as a source of sadness than to see it as a blessing. Even the young who wait impatiently for the fullness of their adult powers and opportunities must experience sorrow, as time takes away from them much that they love. The rest of us have no difficulty in identifying with the mood of a popular song which looked back at youth and said, "Those were the days, my friend. We thought they'd never end." But they did end. They always do end. In our most happy times we forget about endings, so absorbed are we in the now-moment of present experience. When the good time is gone we feel the nostalgic longing and it is then that we wish we could slow down the clock in order to extend the period of our joy. We are like the fellow in another song, popular a number of years ago, who was sitting at the organ playing, without paying strict attention to the process, when his hands happened to strike a chord that sounded like musical perfection; but then he moved his hands and he could not remember how he did it. The lyric of the song goes on to describe the frantic, fruitless search for the lost chord, but I wonder what the fellow would have done if he had found it again. Would he have glued his fingers to the keys? If he had, I think we could agree that he would soon have been driven mad by the chord that in a moment of idle transition had seemed heavenly in its perfection.

Like the beauty of music, the beauty of life is in the flow of transformation. Every now and then we experience moments of complete fulfillment. So wonderful are such occasions that if we could halt the flow of time we would do so there and then. Luckily we are unable to do so, for in frozen perfection we would be driven mad by monotony. The preciousness of the moment is due in part to the fact that it is just so at the time of present awareness and will never be exactly repeated again.

Without having given it much thought, most of us become aware of this with the accumulated experience of maturity. Hence in our later years our wish is not to stop time, but rather to slow it down a bit. Older people rightly perceive that only the very young wish their life away by longing for tomorrow instead of savoring the richness of today. In later years we are more aware of the approaching end of our role in the drama of earthly history. For many of us this terminal point becomes a sign of frustration because we have failed to find fulfillment for our dearest hopes. With each passing year we know there is less hope that our best dreams will come true— or, if they do come true, there will be less time to enjoy them. If we survive beyond the middle years of life all of us have some sensitivity to this dark side of time.

But there is a bright side of time, too. For time, like every other differentiation of the Self of the Universe, is the interplay of opposites. Time is a coming-to-be as well as a passing-away. It is tomorrow as well as yesterday. The loneliness that rises out of memory and the sadness that comes from unfulfilled hope can often be matched by eager anticipation of an event that we expect in the not-too-distant future. Planning for a trip is often as pleasant as the actual journey. While saving for the new possession, one may enjoy the fantasy owning of it—a dream that sometimes far exceeds the pleasure of the reality.

Furthermore, the very fact that we do not have forever and are therefore forced into choices enhances the worth of much that we do. After we have grown a bit older we become conscious that there is less time left. When this awareness grows in us, the days become more precious and our choices more significant. Most of us become more wisely cognizant of what we really want in our remaining years, and there are many individuals who have the courage to live in terms of new values that they have discovered, precisely because they are in the later stages of their life. For these people there comes a sense of fulfillment that grows out of the experience of mature years. They can bear witness to the fact that for the loving who are loved, old age can be among the best parts of a lifetime. As in all space/time existence, the brightness casts a shadow and out thoughts about tomorrow are flawed by knowing that we will inevitably lose the embodiments of those we love in this world. However, that necessity becomes less worrisome as we become more sensitive to the eternal One who is the reality of the many.

But the philosophy of panentheism has more to say about time than is found in any attempt to balance the moods of nostalgia and hope. As he comes to increasing understanding of the One-in-all and the all-in-One, the wise person hopes to grow in sensitive appreciation of this differentiated unity in all the various aspects of his experience. This hope involves his feelings about time as well as about other kinds of experience.

Our traditional Western images of time fail to give as much

feeling of temporal unity as do some of the images used by Oriental philosophers. In our tradition, time is pictured as a flowing stream, a moving ribbon, or an arrow in flight. Like the film on a motion picture projector, time unrolls from the unknown future, passes the lens of the projector where for an instant it becomes "now," and then is rolled upon the spool of the changeless past. Such images of time as a linear sequence are derived from Western fascination with language as the indispensable medium for our highly prized intellectual knowledge.

This becomes apparent when you compare the experience of seeing with the process of verbal description of what has been seen. Seeing is an all-at-once experience. The scene has a focal center of attention and it fades off in less distinct edges, but it is all there at a glance. It is a "now" happening rather than a sequential happening. But in order to describe what is thus taken in all at once the experience must be translated into a series of words that follow one after another in temporal sequence.

In our culture there is general agreement that to know something is to be able to put it into words. In our educational systems the capacity to verbalize is the test of knowledge. If you cannot write a good examination you cannot pass the course. Thus we are conditioned to prize intellectual knowledge above carnal knowledge. By magnifying the one and diminishing the other we tend to lose touch with the seamless "now" of present consciousness that is continuously evolving into new experiences. Our habit is to slice up the "now," package it in verbal symbols on the assembly line of grammar, and then we assume that time, like the words in our description of it, is a linear sequence of separate items. So much is this a part of our way of conceiving of time that it is difficult to picture any other way of experiencing it.

To get the feeling of a different image of time, suppose that you are sitting quietly on the summit of a hill with an unbroken view of the west, and you are watching a magnificent sunset. You can see many large clouds blown by the winds of the upper atmosphere into continuously changing shapes. As the sun sinks toward the horizon the color of these various cloud forms is continuously different. From moment to moment the scene is subtly new. Yet, in your still contemplation of the scene, there is no awareness of any "stream," or moving river of time. The differences you are watching do not come from some unknown place in the future, flow past the present, and depart into some place in the past. They simply arise and fade away as changes come and go in the continuously present sky.

It is such an image of time, as a flow of transformation that takes place within an eternal now, that is consistent with the philosophy of panentheism. The Self of the Universe is, in one aspect of his being, the continuous present of the unfolding process of creation. He is the coming-to-be and the fading away of all forms in the universe, and he is also the ever-present continuum in which the total process takes place.

Such a description is, of course, verbal and therefore intellectual. The wise person is one who gets the theory out of solitary confinement in his head and lets it become a motivating power in all of his life. To do this he must come to the realization that in his own experience he lives in a continuous present, just as the Creating Power does in the limitless extension of his being that is not involved in the game of becoming a universe. "Now" is all the time you ever did have or ever will have.

Thus to assert the prime reality of the continuous present does not mean that the past and the future are unimportant illusions. They are real enough, but only as present reality. Both memory and anticipation are "now" experiences, and they can never be anything else.

Suppose, for instance, you think of a meeting that you attended last year. Surely that meeting was real, and it is in the past. But the fact is that what you are *now* experiencing as you think about the meeting is not the actual gathering, but memories of it that you can call up into your *present* awareness. Your memories are echoes of the event which still reverberate in the energy field of your consciousness. No matter how vivid the memory, there is no way that you can go back and participate again in what has faded out of the present.

Even if you captured the scene on television tape so that you could run the tape at a later date and see and hear what once took place, you are not lifted thereby out of the present and into the past. Your viewing is still a "now" experience. The tape, as an energy system, may have a better memory than you of your participation in that meeting, but it cannot change the events that then took place. You cannot step back into the scene and change your vote on some important issue. Only in the now of present awareness is there living transformation.

What is true of the past in relation to the present is also true of the future. We can fantasize in our "now" about what will happen tomorrow. Sometimes we do it in dread, and sometimes in eager anticipation. But we cannot make coming events anything more than symbols in our head until they become the now in which we are living. A limited amount of planning is worthwhile, but after having done what we reasonably can to avert or control tomorrow's expected disaster, it is a mark of a person's trust, generated by realization of truth, to be able to turn away from the future and concentrate on today.

Folk wisdom tells us not to cross our bridges until we get to them. It seems to me that this saying is most often used in relation to negative expectations. However, I feel that it applies also to positive future events. A little imagination brought to bear on things you hope for can go a long way. Too much of it leads easily to the tragic sacrifice of present happiness on the altar of tomorrow.

I once knew a man who so concentrated his financial resources on the possibility of being able to give his family the best of everything "someday," that he spent practically nothing on his wife and children in the early years of their marriage. He salted his money away in the bank. His children grew to hate him. His wife divorced him. He died of a heart attack when he was only thirty-five years old. His golden tomorrow never came. General human observation of such people leads to the conclusion that even if it had come, he wouldn't have recognized it. He would have been planning already for a more magnificent tomorrow, and it would have meant little to him that he had achieved the goal that he had set for himself when he got married.

Since "now" is all the time you ever had or ever will have to live in, my advice is to become skillful at playing it by ear. I mean by this expression that one should aspire to become so exquisitely sensitive to the changing flow of patterns in your present scene that you are able to respond adequately and spontaneously play your part in the unfolding situations.

The ideal is like that of being a trumpet player who is so sensitive to the patterns of flowing harmony in the orchestra that he can play along with the other instrumentalists even though he has no musical score in front of him. That may sound like an impossible ideal, but it was commonly done by the early jazz musicians. They called it "winging it." One of them would take off from the written score and the others in the group would follow, holding the harmony and rhythm together by sheer sensitivity to one another's unfolding patterns of musical behavior. It can also be done in life by those who have a feeling for the continuities of melody, harmony and rhythm that run through our days.

A sense of tempo is very important in playing by ear. One learns to flow with the dance. To clutch at the beat and try to slow it down so as to prolong the goodness only leads to the feeling that the opposite has happened and that the clocks are racing. Conversely, to attempt to make time fly only emphasizes the slowness with which it drags its cast-iron butt across the hours of the day.

When we are totally with it we get neither of these sensations. Our best moments are as timeless as is the movement of a dancer who flows with the beat while being quite unconscious of any attempt to do so. The greatest hours of our lives are a total now-experience in which clocks are forgotten and we move with the vibrations of a heartbeat at the center of creation. Neither memory nor anticipation come in to report their messages of joy or sorrow. We are in total union with some other—a group of people joyously sharing a celebration —an activity in some solitary natural place far from human company—enraptured by a work of art—lost in exquisite union with one whom you dearly love. In any case it comes through being lifted out of your limited self into identity with a larger whole and hence into greater awareness of the Self of the Universe as the inwardly shared source of all existence. When we feel ourselves to be an isolated, tight little ego in an alien environment we are most vulnerable to the dark side of time. When we know ourselves as one with our environment or in an intense unity with any part of our environment we suffer least from temporal transformation.

Our capacity to join in the dance of creation is enlarged as we become more aware of the One by loving the many. It is spontaneously natural for the lover to pay attention to whatever he loves. Lovers find endless fascination simply in looking at one another's faces and gazing into each other's eyes. The wider and deeper and more intense our loving, the greater will be our response to and involvement with our environment. We will forget ourselves through our interest in what is going on, forget ourselves into identification with the everlasting One in whom yesterday and tomorrow are aspects of forever—colors that flash in the turning jewel of the eternal.

BEING SOMEPLACE

Have you heard the story about the jealous husband who came home early from the office to search his house and who found a man hiding in his wife's closet?

"What are you doing in there?" demanded the husband.

"Everybody has to be someplace," explained the embarrassed boyfriend.

I can't imagine that such an explanation gave much satisfaction, but still it was a true statement. To be embodied is to be located in a specific place in both time and space. This kind of necessary limitation, like all the others, can be both a source of pleasure and a source of pain. We have already called attention to the crucial difference it makes in a person's life to be born, for example, among the Eskimos as compared with being born in the African jungle or in Dallas, Texas. In his great play *J. B.*, which is a modern version of the content of the biblical Book of Job, Archibald MacLeish presents, in a kind of prologue, two characters who want to recreate that magnificent ancient poem. One of the two asks where they can find someone to play the part of Job, and the other says that there is always someone playing the part of Job—innocent people who suffer because they are at the wrong place at the wrong time: Hiroshima, Dresden, Pearl Harbor, Pompeii.

Those of us who are city dwellers may be more sensitive to problems of too many people in too little space than are those who live in areas with wide horizons. We are witnesses of the deterioration of the quality of life as the quantity of people crowded together increases. The Planned Parenthood organization distributes an effective bumpersticker that says, "Can't find a parking space? Support Planned Parenthood." The inconvenience mentioned is trivial, but it is symptomatic of countless ills that make urban people generally more aware of the dangers of overpopulation than are rural people. Being sensitive to the amount of space needed by people for good living leads city-bred people to support measures that decrease the rate of growth in population: young couples deciding to have no more than two children (a "replacement family"); free and easily available contraceptive information and devices; programs of education in human sexuality that will tend to produce greater personal responsibility through choices based upon knowledge; sterilization when requested by individuals; public information to dispel false beliefs about male vasectomies; provision for legal abortion as a decision made by a woman and her doctor during the first four months of pregnancy. While it is perfectly true that various subcultural groups in any urban environment will share a general subjective consensus that condemns all of the above measures as immoral, they will be a minority in crowded cities whereas in rural areas they are often a majority. This is but one small example of how values vary according to place.

Overcrowded conditions in city slums constitute an evil experienced by millions of people together. Another kind of unhappiness is experienced when there is too much space between the self and the other. Everybody has to be someplace, and often when two people need each other, because of a powerful emotional attachment or to accomplish some kind of interpersonal transaction, the distance between the place where one is and the place where the other is can cause real distress. The supersonic passenger plane is a symbol of our continuing struggle to diminish the handicaps we feel by our limitation to a single spatial location. Our relentless quest for ever-increasing speed, with the resulting deterioration of the general environment and with slaughter on the highways, is visible evidence of our efforts to overcome evils that arise because there is too much space between places. In this space/time world, any device that shortens travel-time diminishes the effects of distance. We might also note that high-speed travel is the privilege of the affluent. The whole world is your neighborhood if you have money to pay the plane fare. Such increasing disparity between rich and poor in the matter of the availability of distant places is another example of how solutions to problems generate other problems.

Our restriction to a single space/time location results in other difficulties. For instance, I am the rector of a large downtown church and I find myself continually trying to distinguish between people it is important for me to see and people it is urgent for me to see. Such are the limits of my spatial location that often I am forced to neglect the former. So frustrating is this at times that, like others whose obligations are beyond the reach of their possibilities, I wish I could develop a split personality and then carry the division so far that I would become two people. Imagine being able to be in two places at the same time! But such a miracle will not happen. Being someplace necessarily involves not being somewhere else. So the end of the day will continue to bring with it at times the painful awareness that I haven't been able to do all that I wanted. Such awareness is another aspect of the suffering that rises out of the space between.

More is involved here than the inability to be in two hospitals at the same time. The limitation of spatial presence often causes us to imagine that if we had only been with some loved person in their time of crisis we could have prevented some disaster from happening. "If I had only been there I would have . . ." we say. But we can't be everywhere.

The space-between can sometimes be a factor in tragedy even when it is only a matter of a few feet that separates two people trying to communicate with one another. Being unable directly to experience the mind of the other, they are dependent upon audible and visible signals from the solitary confinement of the one to the solitary confinement of the other. The degree of such isolation varies with the amount of love between the two. Lovers who are sensitive to the unity that encompasses their separateness have less difficulty in bridging the gap in meaningful communication than do persons who face each other in an atmosphere of hostility. Yet there are ways in which lovers feel more deeply than others the frustration of particular location. Lovers long for as much unity as is possible. Every happiness feels incomplete unless the other is there to share it. Every sorrow is more hurtful if the other is not there to bring comfort and support. Each longs so to identify with the other that the pleasures and pains of either one are the experience of both. But the hunger for such union is never completely satisfied.

These are a few of the unhappy consequences of our limitation to a particular place. But the philosophy of Panentheism informs us of the necessity of mutual opposition in our experiences of good and evil. It reminds us that the dark side of spatial limitation is a condition that makes possible values that would be unknown to us without it. The good and evil of the space-between are not separate antagonists, but rather they are variant aspects of the unified activity of the Self of the Universe.

The simple fact that you cannot be in two places at once makes possible a precious gift that you alone can give to others, namely your own bodily presence. When a busy person comes to see you, it is obvious that he or she has chosen to be with you rather than to be some place else. If that person could be in fifty places at the same time, then the choice to visit you would be far less significant. It would be something like the television star who thanks you on his program for letting him "visit in your home." The gracious words fail to make personal an appearance that happened in two million homes at the same time.

In my downtown church the teaching that I give from the pulpit each Sunday is broadcast on a powerful radio station. This makes it convenient for members of the congregation to stay home and listen rather than to drive into the city. Thus it is all the more meaningful when members of the parish come to be with the rest of us in the church building on a Sunday morning. The person who actually comes to the church makes a gift of his personal presence—a gift that no one else can make for him, and one that means a great deal to the clergy and the others who are there. The fact that you cannot be everyplace at once makes the choice of where you choose to be a meaningful kind of good.

The chief reason why your bodily presence is valuable is because it is a scarce commodity. There are an infinite number of places where you are not as compared with the one place where you are. We have noted that one of the disvalues that arise out of being someplace is that so often you are absent from some location where one you love is in real need. But suppose that you could be with everyone that you love, is there any certainty that your presence could convert every disaster into triumph? Each of us has his or her own human limitations and most of the time they appear to be commensurable to the events and situations for which we can assume some responsibility in our own location and its close environment. To be in more than one place without a corresponding increase in our ability to cope would simply burden us with increased feelings of guilty inadequacy. To try to do everything is to succeed in doing nothing.

Just as our ability to live wisely in the "now" is largely dependent upon our ability to trust the Creating Power for the future, so our ability to live in the "here" without useless anxiety is dependent upon our confidence that the infinite One knows better than we do what is "best" for those we love who are far distant from us. This is not always apparent. Most of us imagine that we could do a far better job at writing the script for the drama of history than is done by the Self of the Universe. Hence, if we are to have the ability to trust him we need something more than theoretical abstractions as the foundations of our faith. Carnal Knowledge of the One derived from intense and inclusive loving and from mystical experience is needed to give confidence strength and durability.

It seems to me that most of our proposed revisions of the nature of things would lose as much as they would gain for us. We can complain about how the space-between makes communication difficult, even between two people in a face-to-face situation, but think what it would be like if it were possible to tune in on each other's inmost thoughts so that the thinking of each would be perfectly reproduced in the subjective awareness of the other. Gone would be all personal privacy. I shudder to think what it would be like to be with another person who was completely aware of each fleeting whim, each momentary urge, each impulsive thought in my mind. I place a high value on mental privacy and I feel sure all other people feel the same way. While it is true that perfect extrasensory perception carried to the limit would make communication more efficient, it is also true that efficiency is prized by those who place a higher value on productivity than they do on living. Efficiency is often the twin of monotony. Life is very often inefficient and unpredictable. Hence it carries a continuing element of surprise and of challenges to cope with difficult situations.

The space-between blocks the desire of lovers to be one, yet the embodiment that limits us to a single space/time location is also the very essence of the differences between the two—and as the proverbial Frenchman says, *"Vive la différence!"* It is painful to feel at times as if you were the bleeding half of a single divided whole, but without that strong feeling of incompleteness there could be no ecstasy of union on those beautiful occasions when all the differences seem to fit into a single joyous completeness.

Furthermore, the separation between those who love is never absolute, for the experience of loving teaches the two that they are variant forms of a single all-inclusive life. This truth comes into vivid awareness in precious times of intense bodily togetherness. I also think it reasonable to hope that such experience of union will find a full consummation when the roles that lovers play in this time/space existence are dissolved and they awaken fully to the realization that both are truly one in the limitless unity of the Creating Power.

There is also another way in which the space between those who love is a much less than absolute barrier. The one Life that they share is the same Life that shapes and animates everything that exists. So their life is never a totally private affair or a one-to-one relationship only. Knowing the unity of all existence through their loving, they can realize that the qualities to which they respond in the loved one are part of the substance of all animate and inanimate forms on earth.

Do you remember the words of a popular song that went, "I'll be seeing you in all the old familiar places that this heart of mine embraces all day through . . ."? The fact is familiar to lovers and it is easily explained in terms of Panentheism. Since it is true that in loving any other person we are loving the Creating Power, we can feel ourselves in some aspect of the presence of the one we love most whenever we respond with affection to some other person, place or thing. Whatever we embrace with our heart calls forth some precious reminder of our most dearly loved.

This truth is well illustrated in one part of the classic book for children called *The Little Prince*, by Antoine de Saint-Exupéry. In the course of the story the Little Prince tamed a fox so that he was a one-and-only boy in all the world for the fox and the fox was a one-and-only fox for the Little Prince. The relationship was most happy until the time for parting inevitably came and then the little fox began to cry. The Prince said he thought it might have been better if he had never tamed the fox, but the fox said that though he didn't want the Prince to leave, he knew that he would never be completely alone again, for the color of the ripe grain in the wheat fields would always remind him of the color of the Little Prince's hair.

As I have learned to respond with love to the Self of the Universe in people I love, I have discovered that my whole life is lived in an atmosphere of those most dear to me. Such is the universal experience of lovers. The ripple of wavelets along a beach are the sound of her laughter. The curve of a gull's wing is the graceful curve of her body. The sky borrows color from his eyes. An oak embodies his strength. He is the banks of firm rock, while she is the dancing stream that can flow freely because he holds her. He is the boisterous wind kicking up dust and leaves. She is the bird riding effortlessly on the breeze. She is the glowing hearthfire. He is the warm comfort that surrounds the glow.

The space between those who love is still a poignant reality, but it is not nearly as difficult to bear for those who are able to look upon all that is around them with eyes made luminous by loving.

It is in terms such as these that the philosophy of Panentheism helps us to make sense out of the problem of evil. Having done away with the traditional image of a god who is the external spectator of our pain, we come to the realization that the Self of the Universe is the One in the many, the Same in all differences, the Life of all existence. Scientific understanding of the universe as a unified field of a single substance; mystical awareness of the universe as the manifestation of a single, infinite, personal One; and loving sensitivity to the truth that each of us shares a single Life with all other animate and inanimate things—all of these modes of consciousness converge in perceiving that the Creating Power feels in his own personal being all of our individual pleasures and pains as his own. He accepts the terrible dark as part of his own experience in being a universe so that he may also delight in brightness. The tensions and mutual interdependence of opposites are the very stuff of living. It is impossible to imagine a universe without them.

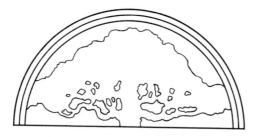

RELIGION IS NOT MORALITY

I wish that my house had a floor.
I don't so much care for a door;
  But this walking around
  With my feet off the ground
Is becoming a bit of a bore.

Those few lines express something of the way I feel when I read some books about morals—sort of floating around in airy abstractions without touching the solid earth where people live. That sort of thing bothers me, for it is contrary to the earthy quality of the philosophy of Panentheism. Although the Self of the Universe is more than anything that we mean when we talk about "nature," he is also identical with nature. In such a way of understanding human experience there is no room for supernaturalism and the morals are as earthy as the religion. Yet it is important to differentiate between the two, as one seeks to practice a meaningful style of life rooted in contemporary knowledge of reality.

We have already noted that a first-century writer called James, who is included in the pages of the Bible, defined true religion as morality. He said that "true religion" is to visit widows and orphans in their affliction and to keep oneself "unspotted from the world." In other words, he thought that the religious man is one who practices works of mercy and helpfulness toward the poor and needy and who rejects the fun and games practiced by his worldly neighbors. James was

117

not the only one who thus viewed religion as another name for morality. Several other biblical passages support such an interpretation. In the parable of the "Sheep and the Goats," for example, we are told that the good sheep will be welcomed into Paradise while the wicked goats will be sent to roast forever in Hell. The parable indicates that the difference between the two is that the good sheep fed the hungry, gave drink to the thirsty, welcomed the stranger, clothed the naked, and visited those who were confined by illness or imprisonment. The wicked goats are sent to damnation not for any positive wrong but rather for sins of omission. They failed to do what the sheep did. So this teaching also seems to indicate that religion is concerned with morally approved behavior and nothing else. Do good things in order to win the reward of Heaven and avoid the punishment of Hell.

It is common thus to consider religion a matter of good behavior and hence to think that morality is the religion of the saints. This is, however, the reverse of the truth. Efforts to imitate the way of life of the saints by strenuous obedience to moral rules will end in frustration and bitterness. Their religion is not the result of their morality. Quite the opposite: their morality is the result of their religion. Preachers tend to miss the most significant part of the parable of the Sheep and the Goats. It is found in the following words of Jesus: "Forasmuch as you have done it unto one of the least of these my brethren you have done it unto me." Here is a clear indication that Jesus of Nazareth shared in the Panentheistic experience of the world, for he knew that there is one life in all people and through his loving he identified with what happened to any other person. The exhortation to be a sheep rather than a goat misses the essential point. The heart of the parable is to share the viewpoint of the Nazarene. Be a loving person and the rest will follow.

Those who interpret religion as a matter of promises made to the "good," and threats of punishment aimed at the "wicked," can easily convince the people in the pews that religion is morality motivated by a carrot and a club. In our culture this message is generally heard as a kind of good news, for most of our people feel that they conform reasonably well to the moral standards of the community in which they live. They may not be perfect, but then neither are any of their neighbors—and isn't it true that the Lord is merciful and forgiving? Indeed, in our day of television news it is not difficult to persuade yourself that you are very much better than other people. Day after day you watch a parade of nasty characters on your TV screen who have done things that you fancy you would never do. So it is easy to believe that you no longer need to be coaxed and scolded into righteousness on Sunday mornings. You're doing all right and you can forget church and go out for a round of golf.

What passes for morality in most of these people is little more than habitual conformity. They do what is expected of them without thinking about it. It seems to me that we might well call their behavior "proper" rather than "moral," for a moral action is one that is motivated by a feeling of obligation and is in conformity with some personally acknowledged standard of behavior. A man is being moral when he seriously considers a course of action that may be inconsistent with his feelings of what he should do, and then, with some awareness of reluctance, pushes himself to do something different because it is, in his culturally conditioned system of values, the "right thing to do." I see no point in calling an action moral when a person does it because it never occurs to him to do anything else. Yet in the complexities of interrelated values there is something good and important about such dull and predictable propriety. Every community needs a powerful group of unimaginative conformists to provide stability to the social situation. They play a very necessary role in the drama of the Creating Power. They are, so to speak, the chorus that stands in the background and comments on the action, thus providing a sense of continuity and a feeling of stability as vivid contrast with the actions of the principals. Without such common obedience to moral conventions, we would all be in big trouble. They have generally evolved out of centuries of human experience in learning both how to minimize conflict and how to increase cooperation in a group for the good of all the members. If you can't give the other fellow a break because you love him, then it is a fairly good substitute to do so because your culture has conditioned you to feel that you ought to.

As a follower of the religious philosophy of Panentheism I maintain that religion is not concerned with what *ought* to be or what *should* be. Religion is concerned with what *is*. Since the Self of the Universe is present in all forms of existence I consider religion to be a matter of experiences, attitudes, and actions that have their source in a loving response called forth by sensitivity toward whatever is directly or indirectly present to consciousness. Religion is not conformity to commands supposedly given by past authorities. Neither is it an attempt to force oneself to live up to some future ideal of what one may become. In simplest terms, religion is life motivated by love for any part of the scene around the self. It has nothing to do with "doing your duty."

It may help to see how this is so if at this point I review again the fundamental principles of Panentheistic understanding. I remind you, then, that the unity of the whole creating process as described in modern scientific theory is an "outsider's view" of what we, on the inside of our particular subordinate system of vibrations, know to be the self-expression of the limitless Self of the Universe, who is at least personal since we, as persons, are forms of his/her being. We are using a human metaphor when we speak of the infinite One as personal and call the One the "Self of the Universe" or the "Creating Power." The fact is that we can only think and communicate in human terms, so there is no way adequately to express what the intrinsic nature of the One may be. We are only asserting by our use of personal terms that the dynamic field or continuum of self-evolving forms is not mindless mechanism or random happenstance.

Since the single, limitless, creating Life is as much the self of the human knower as it is the self of that which he knows we cannot realize its presence as an object. We know the Creating Power only through our awareness of unity between the self and the other, and this realization that we two are one is a kind of carnal knowing that is discovered in mature loving. The lover feels deep in the vital center of his being that his life is not an isolated possession, but rather that it is one configuration of a larger life that includes those he loves as other configurations of the same reality.

In his most intense loving he knows that his beloved is, in a lover's metaphor, "the other half of myself." He is thus aware of the One who is also the many. His experience confirms the literal accuracy of the ancient biblical saying: "He who loves knows God." Or to say the same thing in the terms of Panentheism, "He who loves knows the Self of the Universe." And this is why I say that religion is the experience of loving and spontaneous actions that flow from loving. It is not obedience to a moral code.

This distinction between moral action and religious action is often very subtle but nonetheless discernable. Take, for example, the giving and receiving of gifts. To the outside observer it would appear to make no difference whether the motivation of the giver is love or a sense of moral obligation. Those involved in the transaction know better. The lover, spontaneously doing what he wants to do, so identifies with the recipient of the gift that he shares her pleasure. He feels enriched by his giving, for the delight of the one who receives an offering of love is equally the delight of the one who gives. The worth of his gift lies dormant in consciousness until it is passed to the one he loves. Then in the transfer from one part of his self to another part of himself, so to speak, the hidden value becomes luminous. The gift becomes a source of enjoyment rather than a mere possession.

The moral man, on the other hand, tends to measure the worth of his act in terms of his experience of suffering caused by his voluntary self-deprivation. "Give till it hurts," is a moral rather than a religious maxim. The motivation for giving is self-centered rather than other-centered. The moral man feels that he ought to assist the weak and the poor. He feels guilty if he fails to do so. His internalized voice of authority from his past scolds him for being selfish. The same voice commends him when he does what he should do. He feels that he is "good" if he gives, and the more he dislikes parting with his possession the more internal credit he receives from his internal judge. For the moral man the act of giving carries no intrinsic happiness, but it does enable him to avoid the discomfort of guilt and to obtain the satisfaction of self-approval.

I want to point out, however, that though I have, for the sake of clarity, spoken as though the moral person is necessarily a different person from the religious person, in actual circumstances of living no such sharp division is common. I suppose that at the extremes of the mutual interplay of religion and morality there may be some people who are almost completely motivated by love and others who are almost completely motivated by obligation. But most of us are in the middle of the curve of normal distribution: sometimes moral, sometimes religious, and often half one and half the other at the same time. The most loving person will often turn for guidance to the ethical tradition of his cultural group. The most moral person will occasionally act out of pure love.

While it is obvious that I write as one who places a higher value on the lover than on the moralist, I recognize that the moralist serves a very specific function in any social system. He is the guardian of order. Acting in terms of inherited traditions of behavior, he maintains the patterns of human interaction that have public approval, so that people know what to expect from one another. Morality serves the same function as rules of the road in driving an automobile. Traffic can only flow smoothly when everyone generally follows the same regulations. If choosing which side of the street you wish to use were a new and arbitrary decision each time you sat behind the steering wheel the result would be chaos and bloody disaster. Note, also, that no amount of loving could be an adequate substitute for such rules. It might even make matters worse if two saintly drivers stopped at an intersection and one declined to proceed before the other: "After you, Pierre." "No, after you, my dear Gaston!" As an automobile driver the loving person will be one who realizes the importance of obedience to the rules of the road. Similarly in general life the loving person will see the importance of moral standards. He will support them and tend to live by them.

As a Panentheist, however, he will not confuse his morality and his religion. With all the limitations of his first-century way of thinking, even old St. Paul was aware that the most spectacular acts of unselfishness are not the stuff of religion if they are done without love. You may remember that in his famous thirteenth chapter of his first letter to the people in the Greek city of Corinth he wrote, "If I give away all my possessions, and if I deliver my body to be burned, but I have not love, I gain nothing."

That last phrase—"I gain nothing"—is a reflection of a religious accounting system in terms of which most everyone seemed to think in those days. It means that an action done without love, no matter how great the sacrifice, accumulates no credit toward the price of a ticket to Heaven after your death. Disregarding such pious economics, it seems clear that St. Paul was aware that love is the heart of religion, even though he did not recognize the inconsistency between loving action and action motivated by hope of reward or fear of punishment. The deed that is done as a way of earning admission into Heaven, or one that is done as a way of avoiding eternal punishment in Hell, is self-centered in its motivation. It is a way of getting "me" into pleasure and keeping "me" out of pain. Such appeals to self-interest are often effective ways of controlling conduct, but behavior thus motivated is a long way from loving action motivated by awareness of the personal self and the self of the beloved as variant forms of the limitless Self of the Universe.

Religion that is thus centered in knowing the One in our experience of loving will not be manipulative. The message is not one of using love as a means to some further goal. We do not say that a person should love in order to win Heaven and avoid Hell. The value of loving is intrinsic rather than extrinsic. The lyric of a song that was popular in a previous generation expresses this truth in a clear and simple way: *Not for hair so golden. Nor for eyes of blue. Not because you're fair, dear. Not because you're true. When you ask the reason, words are all too few. Can't you see I love you just because you're you.* In short, the lover can give no reason for his loving. If he could, it would not be love in the most mature meaning of that word.

Genuine lovers will, of course, make the attempt to say why they love. He may say, "I love you because you have blue eyes and golden hair," but this may simply be another way of saying, "I love you—all that you are including your beauty, in which I take delight." Blue eyes and blond hair are not really the reason for his loving. After all, such colors are not the unique possession of his beloved, and he doesn't love every blue-eyed blonde he meets. He could just as well say, "I love you because you are a brown-eyed blonde," if that is what you are, and it would simply mean, "I love you because you are you." Not "I love you because you are beautiful," but rather, "You are beautiful to me because I love you."

This reminds me that sometimes I think it would be pleasant

to form an organization called People Resisting Old Sayings. Elderly members of the group could then call themselves by the acronym for the group. They would be "old PROS" and their effort would be to rid the world of traditional nonsense such as the maxim that informs us that "love is blind." The truth is quite the opposite. Indifference and dislike are blind. Those who feel no affection toward a particular person will be unaware of the worth of that person and hence they will wonder how it is that someone else loves him or her. Assuming the accuracy of their own perception, they will describe the attitude of the one who cares by saying that love is blind. The truth is that love sees, for every person on earth is of intrinsic worth as the self-expression of the Creating Power.

But if the one who cares for you is not sensitive to that intrinsic worth; if his "reasons" for loving you are more than expanded ways of repeating, "I love you," then you had better consider the possibility that he is in some way using you for his own advantage. The fellow who says, "I love you because you give me a thrill," or " . . . because you are a great cook," or " . . . because dating you gives me status on the campus," is really concerned about his own pleasure and his own ego. He is the sort of man who looks for credit as a lover of people when his real purpose is to earn "pie in the sky by and by when you die."

I like the saint who, in some ancient legend, went around the streets of her city carrying a broom and a bucket of water. When asked why she did it, she explained that the broom was to sweep the gold off the streets of Heaven and the water was to put out the fires of Hell. "Then," she said, "people will have to love the good Lord for Himself alone."

An act of mature love is not compelled by obedience, not pushed by fear of punishment, not pulled by hope of reward. It is simply the free and spontaneous self-expression of the lover. It flows from his vital center as naturally as breathing. It is not so much something that he *does*, as it is something that he *is*. His life is a shared life, and his love is a name for his feeling of unity between himself and others.

In the religious philosophy of Panentheism the lover knows that all of us are subordinate differentiations of a single infinite Life, and that this limitless Life in which we all participate is the life of the Self of the Universe. Hence, whether we acknowledge it or not, the fact is that we love the Self of the Universe in loving any other person, place, or thing.

Religion is not being moral. Religion is being loving.

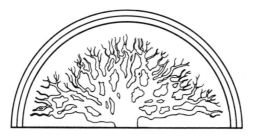

DOING WHAT COMES NATURALLY

"But you can't really mean that being loving is the same thing as being religious. That would make religion a matter of subjective experience. Where are your objective standards? People need to be told what is right and what is wrong. They needs creeds and commandments." Thus spoke a conservative, clergy friend of mine. He is aware of the mutual interdependence of values, at least in so far as being aware that saints need sinners and insiders need outsiders. To make such distinctions clear he felt the need of erecting barriers around membership in a religious group and also around authoritatively defined virtues. Creeds and commandments were his building blocks for erecting a Chinese wall between the acceptable and the unacceptable.

I sympathize with his desire for objective standards, but wishes do not make reality, except among those who agree to play a game of Let's Pretend, in which they will all make believe that the world actually conforms to their shared desires. Apart from such communities of cooperative fantasy, the fact is that all moral values are subjective, whether moralists like it or not. The man who says, "Stealing is wrong," means either, "I disapprove of stealing," or, "The people among whom I live and whose authority I accept as my standard of judgment agree in their disapproval of stealing." He is either reporting the state of his own feelings, or he is giving his estimate of the consensus of subjective feelings of the group with which he identifies himself. The fact that a whole community may agree in their disapproval of stealing does not prove that such a moral judgment is a universal, built-in aspect of human nature, or that moral commands are handed down by a supernatural deity. It is evidence of nothing more than the fact that the members of that community share a common relationship to past generations in which the operating rules of the group were developed out of experience.

Objective morality is like original sin. I once asked members of a college freshman class in Religion to write a brief paper on the doctrine of Original Sin. One clever student turned in a paper in which he said that he and all the friends he knew had spent several hours in serious discussion of the subject. As a result, they were convinced that someone in times past must have tried every possible sin that any of them could think of. So it was his conclusion that there is no such thing as an "original sin."

Similarly, in times past, by somebody at sometime, every evil has been considered good and every good has been considered evil. There is no such thing as an act that always, by everyone in all places, is judged to be wrong. This does not mean that moral values are mere fantasies that are of no importance among people. It means only that they are not delivered to us by some supernatural judge who lives above the sky. As we have already said in previous pages, moral rules are the embodiment of past experience in minimizing conflict and maximizing cooperation in the social and personal relations of a group of people. As social and environmental conditions change, moral rules change, no matter how much such transformation is resisted by conservatives.

Just because moral rules are so important in keeping order in a community, it is easy to overestimate their value. There are occasions and situations when the moral customs of the group will not be allowed to dictate the conduct of the loving.

Hence, the religious person will occasionally be the opponent of the moralist. He will sometimes do what the community judges to be wrong, not in spite of being religious, but for the very reason that he is religious.

We have glimpses of this in the very sketchy records of the life of Jesus of Nazareth. At his time and place in history it was easy for a Jewish husband to divorce his wife. The only requirement was that he hand her a written "bill of divorcement: "I, Peter, divorce you, Hannah." That's all there was to it. She had to leave her husband's house. If she had neither parents nor adult children to look after her, the only way that she could keep alive was by prostitution. Because of such divorce practices there were lots of women on the streets of Galilee and Judaea who were whores, and Jesus was a friend of many of them—a fact which shocked the righteous. He was considered immoral for having such friends. But he was immoral precisely because he was religious.

Not very long ago it was considered the height of immorality for a white woman to marry a black man in many parts of the United States. Granted that the couple might have serious problems unless they could manage to live in a more tolerant part of the world, I am personally convinced that a man and a woman might marry across racial barriers because they are truly religious people—that is, maturely loving. Their religion would lead them to go contrary to the moral judgment of other people. When religion and morality thus collide head on, the howls and scowls of the righteous do little to commend their way of life to others. In such circumstances virtue is very often nasty rather than nice.

During the struggle for civil rights for black people in Baltimore, Maryland, I happened to be the Chairman of the Citizen's Committee for Equal Opportunity Legislation. While holding that office and working to open all places of public service and amusement to people of all races, I received many passionately sincere letters from people who accused me of laboring for an immoral cause. Among these was one that I kept for a souvenir. It ran as follows: *Dear Nigger-lover, If I ever meet you on the street I'm going to give you a good punch in the nose. Sincerely yours, A TRUE Christian.*

Yet, in my own judgment, my actions at that time were an expression of my religion, even though they were contrary to what many people in Baltimore and in the State of Maryland were convinced was proper morality, as ordained by God.

Similarly, I make no apologies for being in favor of eliminating all legislation concerning abortion from the statute books and thus letting the procedure be governed only by standards of good medical practice. This particular difference of opinion illustrates clearly the distinction between morality as obedience to authority and religion as action related to particular present situations and motivated by loving concern for all who are involved. The anti-abortion organizations accept the pronouncements of Papal authority and of the thundering voices of a few conservative Protestant clergymen. Some of us on the other side of the issue feel loving sympathy for the plight of women with unwanted pregnancies.

Our opponents on this issue would refuse to admit that their position is dictated by obedience to past or present authority. Their refusal would generally be sincere since cultural conditioning is largely an unconscious process. They would claim that they also are motivated by love—in this case, by love for the unborn fetus. However, theirs is a peculiar use of the word "love." Obviously it cannot mean what that word means to a Panentheist because there cannot be an honest-to-God feeling of affection in it. I can't imagine how one feels affection for an unborn fetus in the first months of pregnancy, especially one in the womb of some twelve-year-old girl of incomplete education. So in my view (which has no claim to be a pronouncement of absolute truth) the dispute over abortion is, at least in some cases, an example of conflict between moralists and religious people.

Since love is awareness of, and action called forth in response to, the One in the many, our modern religious philosophy lays no great stress on self-discipline. This bothers those who still cling to the religion of the past. They like to sing about themselves as "soldiers of the cross,"—a tightly disciplined band of dedicated heroes "marching as to war." Moralists also like to picture themselves as masters of self-control. They give stern athletic advice to others telling them to "get hold of yourself," and to "exercise your will-power."

The trouble with attempts to force yourself to be good by the practice of continuous self-discipline is that the end product is a lifeless, synthetic conformity that is dead because it lacks a heart. It simply isn't possible to become a saint by painting an idealized self-portrait in pastel colors complete with luminous halo, hanging it in your imagination, and then trying to climb into it.

I remember that Mark Van Doren, the poet, once wrote an essay in which he said that he had made it a rule of his life never to do anything that he really did not want to do. Most people seem to assume that following such advice would produce nothing but antisocial behavior. But, like Mr. Van Doren, I have more faith in my fellow human beings. I know that their ability to love is more or less limited, and that the great majority have little capacity to care for people simply as people without something added to make them appear more attractive. Even so, I feel sure that most people have some ability to feel affection for those beyond the intimate circle of their family, friends, and co-workers. Their positive emotional awareness of persons outside of their own in-group may be limited to certain kinds of others, to white, Anglo-Saxon Protestants for example. Yet it seems to me that there is enough of such limited and qualified emotion around to make most citizens fair and kind in their dealings with others, and not because they have to but because they want to. So I seriously doubt that if it were a universal rule to avoid doing whatever you really do not want to do, everyone would say, "Me first, and to Hell with the hindmost."

There would, of course, be some changes. We might find difficulty in getting "volunteers" to solicit funds for "worthy" causes. It is possible, however, that some of these causes are not really worth supporting and they could be eliminated without social disaster. Others might be better supported in some way other than personal solicitation. In one way or another I am confident that those causes that are truly important would continue to get the money they need. Most of us are aware that some of our institutions, including, to a very large degree, our churches, can be easily caricatured as gigantic mechanical monsters sucking in money that is needed to keep the machinery going so that it can continue to suck in money. Any clergyman can tell you that a very large part of the mail that he gets from denominational headquarters is concerned either directly or indirectly with raising money.

Because the church I serve in downtown Baltimore, Maryland, has been among the top churches of our denomination in terms of the financial support given to the parish by the individual members, people at the national headquarters once wrote to us asking which pieces of their "promotional material" we had used to achieve such a high level of giving. I had to confess that we used none of it. We send out three or four letters, in one of which we include a pledge card asking that it be returned by mail. The few cards not thus returned we pick up in person. Any professional fund raiser can tell you that that is *not* how to do it. Yet it brings results. The reason is simple and also profound: our members and friends care for their parish, and our continuous teaching of relevant, contemporary religion is important in their lives. It is not necessary to twist a person's arm to get him or her to support something that he or she loves.

Life lived in terms of not doing anything that you really do not want to do does not turn out to be a life governed by momentary urges of whim and caprice. At times, when I have been working on this book during my vacation, I have wished that I were out sailing. But this does not mean that I am forcing myself to do something that I do not want to do. It is not unusual for a dominant desire to be in conflict with a subordinate desire. Most of the time when faced with a choice, we have little difficulty in knowing what we really want, and most of the time, I feel sure, that is what we will really do.

Anyway, I'm convinced that most fouled-up people that have come to me for counsel because of their desperate inability to live happily, and at peace with others, are precisely those who have tried to live by self-discipline in accordance with someone else's ideals rather than their own honest inclinations.

Knowing that the unbounded One chooses to become the variety of the many, I have no love for forced conformity. People who live life from their own natural center will be divinely different from each other, as is the intent of the Creating Power. I respect an honest villain more than a synthetic saint. I pity the born musician who tries to become a banker to please his parents, or the sensuous woman who tries to live like a nun, because when she was a child she was conditioned by adult prudery into thinking of sex as the sin most hated by God.

One of my favorite stories is one told by the great Jewish philosopher, Martin Buber. I can't remember the name of the person about whom the story was told, but let's say that it was Rabbi Cohen. The story ends with the Rabbi saying to his disciples, "When I come before the Most High to be judged in terms of what I have done with my life, He isn't going to ask me, 'Why weren't you Moses?' His question will be, 'Why weren't you Rabbi Cohen?'"

I have no doubt that the Self of the Universe can bring forth another St. Francis, or Albert Einstein, any time he wants to do so. The possibility for any role needed in the drama of history is there in the genetic pool. Our task in the drama is to become aware of our own role and play that part as well as we can. The accomplishment of such an aim seems more probable if we avoid doing what we really don't want to do, and if we do what is truly our heart's desire. Our sensitivity to what we really want will obviously involve our responsibilities and our concern for others. Such counsel will not lead to a life of universal approval. No one is admired by all. But I doubt that it will lead to a life of criminal behavior. If in certain situations you are judged to be a villain, remember that sinners sometimes have exciting adventures. Besides, the value of saints is dependent upon the existence of sinners.

In addition to this matter of following the lead of your loves, I want to mention another aspect of this business of accepting your own role in life by living out of the vital center of your personal and unique individuality. It involves emotional as well as intellectual honesty.

This is a subject that must be prefaced with a warning. Honesty of any kind can be, and often is, used as a weapon by the righteous. Telling the truth can do a devastating amount of harm under the cloak of innocence. It is a virtue that stinks sometimes of hatred and revenge, so we should be careful of how we use it. No general rules can be given other than our previous counsel to "play it by ear," keeping in mind the truth that we do not unnecessarily hurt those we love. Neither do we make the mistake, on the other hand, of thinking that we must sacrifice our own authentic being in order to avoid hurting someone else. As I have already pointed out in these pages, mature love is not a you-instead-of-me feeling. Rather, it is awareness of value in union—a we-together feeling. The carnal knowledge of shared life stimulates decisions that include the value both of the lover and of the beloved, neither one being completely dominant or subordinate. Concern for intellectual and emotional honesty takes place within the larger awareness of what is best for both persons.

As I see it, intellectual honesty in religious life for Christians includes acceptance of scientific, historical and literary research as tools for understanding the collection of ancient literature that is called the Bible. Honesty demands interpretation of the meaning of the text in terms of its total context—literary, social and historical. The honest interpreter will not string together a group of biblical sentences selected from unrelated contexts and use them to convince the gullible of the "truth" of his own preconceived ideas. Neither will an honest clergyman pretend that the creeds that he uses as symbols of faith can be taken literally by modern people with any intelligence and education. He will face frankly with his people the evidences of primitive cosmology in such phrases as those that say that Jesus "ascended into Heaven" (i.e., went up to the dwelling place of God above the blue sky) and "descended into Hell" (i.e., went down below the surface of the ground to the place where the devil imprisons and tortures sinners). The small amount of preaching that I am able to hear on Sundays convinces me that the major failing of the clergy is intellectual dishonesty.

Although all of us can recognize the importance of intellectual honesty, I don't think that most of us have been exposed to equal concern about emotional sincerity—that is, about not making a public display to others, or even making believe to yourself, that you feel something that you do not feel. Yet it seems to me that as much harm is done by pretended emotions as is done by intellectual insincerity. Many persons get to be experts at feigning emotions they do not feel in their pursuit of sexual involvement. People pretend to the emotion of love simply in order to get a desired partner to go to bed. Church officials often pretend that they are a kind of reincarnated Jesus with a universal fatherly concern for all of their "beloved brothers and sisters" in the church. The people who are supposed to fall for such synthetic saintliness often are able to see through the smokescreen of pious fraud, but I have found that they often make matters worse by pretending to believe that the official is emotionally honest when they know perfectly well that he isn't. The falsehood is compounded. Then people wonder why the "love" so highly regarded as an ideal in their church seems to outsiders to be so unconvincing if not obviously faked.

Emotional insincerity tends to foul up any kind of interpersonal relationship. Just as parents can teach their children to be dishonest by making them afraid to tell the truth for fear of severe punishment, so all of us can contribute to the emotional insincerity of others by making it perfectly clear that their relationship with us is dependent upon their display of what we consider to be acceptable emotions. The wife who demands the love of her husband is, in reality, making a continuing attack on his emotional integrity. We can control our outward behavior, but it is impossible for any of us by a single act of will to control our emotional life. "You *must* love me" actually amounts to saying, "You must pretend to an emotion that you do not feel, and in all that you say and do you must act as if you love me." By such tactics holy wedlock is transformed into holy deadlock, and a basic relationship of two people becomes an elaborate game of make-believe.

Genuine emotions come only as a spontaneous response to an environment. If you are hoping for a certain emotional response in some other person, the best you can do is to use your intelligence and imagination to create a set of circumstances that are the natural conditions in which the emotion you hope for will be encouraged to grow. There can be no guarantee that the provision of such circumstances will produce the emotional response that you desire, but consider the alternative. We can be certain that when we demand an emotion as a kind of command performance, we will *never* get the genuine article.

Letting other people be emotionally sincere comes easily to people who practice the same permissiveness toward themselves. The moralistic "should" and "ought" have no place in a healthy emotional life. If, for example, you are a person who too easily loses your temper, it does no good to call yourself bad names and to tell yourself that you should not lose your temper. Such self-admonishment only adds guilt to frustration, for the problem of the quick-tempered is the fact that he doesn't know how to control his fits of anger. It is better to accept the fact that you are easily angered, as part of the person you have become through the interaction of your peculiar individuality with your physical and social environment. As a Panentheist such a person will be aware that he, like everything else that exists, is a process rather than a static thing. Behavior engendered by circumstance can be altered by specifically chosen new circumstances of a therapeutic relationship with a trained professional. Meanwhile, whether such a handicap is overcome or not, it is good for each of us to know that we are not alone in having "problems" in our personality structure. All of us have them. They are instances of the way in which the Self of the Universe makes his experience interesting by becoming a variety of imperfect, limited selves in the drama of creation.

Those who follow the philosophy of Panentheism accept the peculiar individuality of their own emotional lives, and at the same time, knowing that they are a process, they expect to grow and change. Thus the person with emotional sincerity is constantly testing the adequacy of his real emotions against the realities of his environmental situation. After you have discovered many times that you were afraid when there was little to fear; after you have alienated others several times by inappropriate anger; after you have been miserable in a relationship that was the consequence of your pretending that your lust was love; after learning by difficult experience those situations and actions that tend to sever the vital connection between your emotional life and the facts of living—then your pain and frustration will naturally stimulate emotional changes for the better. Life is a great therapist, but it can be effective only if you bring your real emotions out into the open and put them to the test of public expression. The practice of emotional sincerity can sometimes be hard on others, but the lack of it can bring on total misery.

THE SPICE OF LIFE

Among the oddities of this world, I treasure the memory of one very earnest missionary whom I met while I was teaching in Wuchang, China. He had been sent to the Orient by one of those only-true-church-of-Christ denominations that seem to flourish in the Western part of the United States. His assignment was to convert missionaries!

Members of his church believed that in all the world they alone had the saving truth. All other creeds were, in their judgment, worse than useless, for they gave to believers a false sense of security. Trusting in an erroneous doctrine, converts would be confident of admission into the divine kingdom of eternal bliss after death, only to discover, when it was too late, that they would be condemned to Hell for believing the wrong things.

This fellow's mission was one of correcting the errors of missionaries so that they would not lead the helpless heathen merrily down the path that leads to damnation. To the degree that any other missionaries did not agree with the one Truth revealed by God to members of his church, it was the solemn conviction of this man that they were instruments of the Devil. They were increasing the future population of Hell.

We people of western culture take great pride in our monotheism. It has been our conviction for many generations that having only one God is the mark of proper ladies and gentlemen. We have been brought up to believe that polytheism is characteristic of childish, primitive natives who do not even know enough to cover their bodies with decent clothing. We have been told that it was our solemn obligation to convert these ignorant savages into Christian consumers of our manufactured goods. By clothing as well as converting the natives our ancestors did well by doing good. We were spreading monotheism.

But our monotheism has a catch in it—one well illustrated by my missionary to missionaries in China. The practical meaning of our monotheistic faith comes down to the statement: "There is only one God—namely, the one in which our particular religious denomination believes. All other versions of monotheism are, to the degree that they differ from ours, false."

The larger, standard-brand churches do not publicly emphasize their conviction that the one God is strictly and exclusively a member of their denomination, but the implication is there, and it is acted on in ecclesiastical strategy. I have been present at high-level meetings of denominational leaders who expressed real concern that people who lived in a particular town had no church to attend. We all knew that there were three churches of other denominations there. But these did not count. The one God is Episcopalian. He wants people to attend "His Church." (I'm not picking on Episcopalians. The same unconscious arrogance can be found in any major denomination.)

One of the amusing things about the kind of monotheism we have spread abroad is the way in which our colossal conceit is practiced in the name of humility. "God has entrusted us with the true faith, and it is our humble duty to share the gift with others." Thus the effort to swell the ranks of the Catholic, or Baptist, or Lutheran, or any other church by converting new members to belief in their creed, and practice of their ceremonies, is publicized as an act of obedience to the will of God.

This can get to be pretty confusing until you come to the realization that there are several "one and only" gods, each of which is the exclusive property of a particular denomination, and each of these gods demands that everyone else be converted to exclusive belief in him.

Come to think of it, though, this is a rather clever move on the part of the Self of the Universe—a way of preserving variety in religion among people who share our kind of culture. Being aware of how people in our intellectual tradition will feel the urge to reduce religious differences to dull uniformity by making everyone worship "the one and only God," the Creating Power arranged for this verbal idol to be published in several different editions. Thus people are free to pursue their ideals of theological uniformity without any danger of reducing delightful variety to homogenized unity.

Of course, when I talk about how the Self of the Universe arranges things, I'm using the intuitive language of myth. Obviously, I don't really know *why* the One behaves in a certain way, but I do know *that* he behaves in a certain way simply by observing the world about me which is the product of his continuous self-expression.

Such awareness of the surrounding scene leads to the assertion that the fundamental observable fact, in the continuously evolving process by which the One becomes the many, is the fact of variety. The Self of the Universe never does the same thing twice. No two people, no two kittens, no two trees, no two rivers, no two sunsets, no two blades of grass, when examined in sufficient detail, are ever exact duplicates of one another. Therefore, it is a reasonable assumption that the Creating Power wills variety, and those who want to cooperate with that Power will work to maintain and increase variations in all the forms of existence. The old religion that we left behind when we came over to the new age of scientific and philosophical understanding proceeded on the opposite assumption. It was a prime article of the faith to claim that it is the will of God that everyone become Episcopalians just like us.

Such apparent perversity had its roots in our traditional high evaluation of intellectual knowledge, almost to the exclusion of carnal knowledge that comes through loving sensory awareness. Intellectual knowledge is words in your head. You "know" something when you have a label for it, with words that define that label in ways that are consistent with some publicly accepted verbal standard. Such definitions are always verbal abstractions. All "women," for example, are grouped under a single definition in the dictionary, but any human being knows that no two of them are alike. Dictionary definitions are also static. They make no allowance for the truth that every "thing" is in reality a process. Intellectual knowledge, being based upon verbal definitions, thus easily leads to attitudes in which differences do not make any difference. Thinking in terms of sameness and paying little attention to the temporal transformation of the processes that we define as things, we tend to place a high value on uniformity, and to see nothing wrong with the attempt to eliminate religious variety in the world.

Only in our face-to-face primary personal relationships, where carnal knowledge breaks up the neat categories of intellectual knowledge, do we realize that differences are truly important. Intense love is always directed toward the unique individuality of the beloved. In contrast with such sensitivity to individual forms and their differences, the urge to convert the heathen is based upon intellect rather than affection. Hence it necessarily deals in collective types rather than in the endless variety of actual existence.

The fundamental intolerance and prideful arrogance of church people is as unconscious as are the roots of prejudice in the general public. Both grow as much from the intellectual bias of our culture as they do from the need of the ego to feel superior to someone else. Destructive prejudice rises out of group definitions passed on in the social group quite apart from any proper empirical test of the validity of the description. It bothers us little that we have almost no personal, direct involvement with the people whom we believe to be evil or inferior. Our knowledge of them is intellectual. We know them in terms of words about words about words, and as proper Westerners we can ask, "What other kind of knowledge is there?" It is for this reason that the attempt to use arguments spun out of intellectual knowledge, as a way of getting rid of prejudice, is mostly a waste of time. We can come down from the cloud-cuckoo land of mental abstractions only by using our capacity for carnal knowledge. Through physical involvement in face-to-face relationships we can come to recognize the stupidity and injustice of prejudice.

Those who in loving the many know that they are loving the One, and who find in this experience their true relation to reality, are sensitive to the importance of differences. Their attitude is not merely that of tolerance. They know that in promoting and prizing variety they are acting in cooperation with the Self of the Universe. So they rejoice in the fact that some of our young people adopt individualistic styles of dress, and they are saddened that so many others have made blue jeans a uniform as rigidly compulsive as any that Adolf Hitler forced upon the youth of Nazi Germany.

Women do a better job of valuing differences in clothing than do men. It is a sound instinct that makes a woman worry lest she be seen in the same dress that someone else is wearing to a particular party. Hopefully, she will pay the same attention to the individuality of all of the rest of her appearance. Making ourselves look as handsome or beautiful as possible is a gift that each of us has to make to others. Since we do not have to look at ourselves we may not mind an unattractive appearance. But others are not so lucky. As the old limerick says: "My face, I don't mind it because I'm behind it; it's the folks out in front get the jar." So I disagree with stringent Puritans who say that efforts spent in making yourself pleasing to look upon are an exercise in personal vanity. Concern for dress and personal appearance is concern for others. No woman puts on her best clothes and grooming simply to spend the day admiring herself in a mirror.

Such efforts at creative self-giving to others involve using intelligence and imagination to express your personal unique individuality. Being attractive in appearance is much more than following whatever may be the current fashion. For some, the latest style may be disastrous, as when some women of more than generous proportions wear slacks or pantsuits although their bodily conformation was never intended thus to be draped. If you've got it, flaunt it. If you haven't got it, fake it. But if you've got too much of it, wear clothing that pleasantly covers it.

If your body was frightened by a famine in a previous in-carnation and is now dedicated to hoarding every ounce of food you eat, you would do well to try to lose some of it, but it is no total disaster if you don't. Some of the most lovable peo-ple I know are pleasingly plump; but then I know others, equally loved, who are mostly skin and bones. When you can-not change some aspect of your bodily presence, accept it as part of your destiny and make the best of it. Appearance is important, but far less important than total personality. Re-member that your particular individuality adds variety to the world, and the Self of the Universe loves variety. The best kind of beauty is that which is apparent to people who love you. The woman who happens to have whatever attributes may be the current fashion for physical beauty in her culture usually finds plenty of men who seek some kind of sexual relationship with her; but she very often misses out on genuine loving.

While clothing and physical appearance contribute to per-sonal affirmation of the importance of differences, they are not all that is involved in authentic individuality, as intended for each of us by the Creating Power. All that I have said in previous pages about such things as moral relativity, living in the here and now, playing your own role in the drama of history, practicing emotional honesty, and the like, are part of the way that you can avoid being a synthetic imitation of other people.

Cooperation with the Self of the Universe in creating and maintaining variety involves more than having the courage to be your real self, and thus different in some ways from all other people. Our life style should be one that supports distinct individuality in other persons and in all of the various groups in which we are involved. Far from seeking to convert others to our own belief and way of life, the philosophy of Panentheism teaches us to take positive pleasure in the ways in which differences in opinion and practices make life more various and interesting.

So what am I doing, writing a book that sets forth my religious understanding in as persuasive a way as is possible for me? Well, the answer is that when you are I you are the kind of person who enjoys thinking about philosophy and sharing his thoughts with others. That happens to be my role or destiny in life. If you happen to agree with what I write, fine. You and I have been so brought forth by the One that we vibrate to the same harmonies. If you disagree with me, also fine. I am not so taken with my own importance that I think that there is any danger that all the world will abandon its variety of philosophical opinion and theological thought and become locked into rigid conformity with my free-wheeling understanding of reality. I'm simply adding to the variety.

This brings up the fact that out of variety very often comes conflict. Followers of the old image of God will surely attack my different opinions, perhaps with bitter antagonism. When opinions vary about things that are important to individuals and groups it is inevitable that they will defend their own views and disparage those they oppose. Such arguments come as no surprise to the person who realizes that the Self of the Universe becomes the multiple selves of people in such a way as to experience the full range of variety. Only out of tensions created by mutual opposition can the values we all treasure arise. For the sake of those values the Creating Power not only tolerates, but actively creates, the conditions of conflict by his mode of becoming a space/time world.

Because limitations are essential to our existence, it is foolish to hope that a time will come when there will be no more competitive struggle among people. Our effort rather should be directed toward possibilities of containing conflict so that it will be less violent and destructive than is often now the case. For instance, we can work for an international code of law under a federal union of all nations upon earth. We can help to promote sympathetic understanding of religious differences. We can try to diminish the violent confrontation of criminals and police, of races, economic groups, classes and nations. Being open to correction while yet supporting the right as we see it, we can hope to increase in ourselves and in others the ability to fight fair in all of our struggles including those that arise in marriage and family life. But contained conflict is still conflict, and so long as there is authentic variety among people there will be antagonistic confrontation.

It is a paradox of the Panentheistic style of life that those who are growing in their capacity to care for all kinds of people and who support with enthusiasm a pluralistic culture characterized by variety of action and opinion are also people who provoke disagreement. They accept their individuality as the intent of the Self of the Universe. They will not abandon it for the sake of peaceful conformity with some dominant majority. Neither will they accept the role of nonentities who mirror the sentiments of any company of the moment. Self-respect involves personal integrity that engenders conflict.

Disagreement that rises out of authentic individuality is

another instance of general truth that we derive our values from the dynamic interaction of opposites. The value of personal integrity comes into conscious awareness in the conflicts that this characteristic of an individual's personality generates. If you stand for nothing at all, you are bound to have enemies who will treat you with contempt as a weakling. You will also have enemies if you express your unique personality in words and action. In the latter case, however, the very fact of arousing opposition makes you vividly aware that you are making some kind of significant contribution to the evolving drama of human history.

The real problem for those who follow the philosophy of Panentheism is to be affectionately tolerant of the opposition while at the same time maintaining the integrity of their own values and judgement. The task is made easier through recognition that each person on earth has a personal destiny. Each of us plays his own part in the drama of history, which is the self-expression of the Creating Power. From your point of view, you are playing the hero and your opponent is the villain. From his point of view, he plays the hero and you are the villain. From the point of view of the Self of the Universe there is no final or absolute hero or villain. If the infinite One were to pass out prizes, my guess is that the individual who played his part with personal authenticity would rate higher than any who claimed a reward on the ground that he or she was victorious in some earthly struggle. Having worked these convictions into the very fiber of my being, I find it much less difficult to deal with my opponents as variant forms of the One.

Granted that such realization does not come easily, I, together with many of my friends, have found that it is altogether possible. Many of us have found that it helps our growth if we can form the habit of looking upon all conflict as moves in a game.

When I take a new person out as a member of the crew of

my racing sailboat I sometimes give a religious test to see if that person is eligible to race with us. Since faith, hope and charity are the three cardinal virtues of Christianity, I ask the prospective crew member if he has faith that we can win; if he hopes that we will win; and whether or not he will feel any charity toward our competitors on the race course. If he says, "Yes," in answer to the first two questions, and something like "Not a damn bit of it," in answer to the third, then he's in. For when I race my boat I play the game hard and I play to win. There's no way, short of intentionally breaking the rules, that I'm going to make it easy for other skippers if I can help it. Yet it is not at all necessary for me to hate my opponents in order to strive for victory. Win or lose, after the race I can have a drink with my opponents and continue to consider them as friends.

Similarly, I find it helpful to cultivate the attitude that my "enemies" in real-life situations are opponents in a game. I take the game seriously and do my best to win, but I have no compulsive need to hate my opponents. They may not have the same attitude toward me. I don't expect it. They know me as an antagonistic person, an irritating individual, a fellow whose dangerous and mistaken ideas must be eliminated for the sake of the purity of Truth. I, on the other hand, know them as variant forms of the One who is the single source of my life and theirs. They sincerely expect to be able to establish an everlasting victory for the Eternal Truth. Such a goal kindles their fanatic zeal. In contrast, I'm aware that the Self of the Universe can use either my victory or my defeat in this particular encounter, as well as the combat itself, to advance his intentions in the unfolding drama of creation. Driven by the unconscious assumption that the universe is a chance collection of transient objects, my opponents tend to feel that absolute issues, life and death, hang on the outcome. Not sharing their illusion, I know that the universe is a dance of the Creating Power, a dramatic game played by the Self of the

Universe who is the source and sustaining life of all the living. When my opponents and I are no longer projected in our present roles in the divine drama, we shall continue in the limitless life of the infinite One.

Such attitudes apply to our personal competitive struggles with other people. We can eliminate hatred from our hearts in our common interpersonal rivalries and differences. It is important to add, however, that within the limits of our human perspective there will always be forms of evil so repulsive as to arouse emotions of antagonistic rejection. Both emotional sincerity and acceptance of our individual role in the evolutionary drama lead us to acknowledge hatred for an Adolf Hitler, a Charles Manson, a Colonel Amin of Uganda. Political terrorists who try to advance their cause by maiming and murdering, bloodthirsty killers of various fanatic groups in North Ireland, the Middle East, Italy and elsewhere, call forth hatred in those who love. People who cause agony and indignity in others are hated in the same way that we hate malignant tumors, birth defects, or starvation. Such hatred in those who recognize the unity of life will not be blind rage. It will be clear-eyed determination to do what one can to eliminate, or deprive of all power to harm, those persons whose actions are so evil, so monstrous, as to pass the limits of compassion and defense. No "explanation" can justify the conduct of these wicked ones. Psychology and sociology can tell us about the causes of their insane cruelty. We can understand sadism, fanatic prejudice and the like. But understanding isn't the point. People who commit unspeakable horrors are to be stopped. Just as our set of opposing values is largely the product of conditions we did not choose, so their condition of wickedness may be due to factors beyond their control. In the mighty drama of creation they have been assigned roles at the extreme opposite of those given to us. Nevertheless, our assigned role is to make humanity safe from their kind. We need feel no guilt about dedicated activity in our role. In our attitudes toward those who cause agony in others, the opposite of hatred, for most of us, is not love. Rather it is hypocrisy—pretending to feel something other than what we actually are feeling. The capacity to care deeply for others includes the capacity to feel revulsion and determined antagonism against those who inflict unspeakable horrors on either animals or people.

Remembering, then, that there are degrees of evil in the behavior of persons and that attitudes appropriate in extreme situations are not applicable to all interpersonal strife, we can find much relief from angry antagonism as the understanding of Panentheism gets out of our head and into our viscera. Someone comes to me raging with anger, sputtering abuse at another person for the terrible thing that he or she did. Why get so hot? It's only a game. Relax and enjoy it. You lost this move, but your turn will come. It is the playing of the game that counts. Do your very best and then accept the outcome. No matter who wins, the results are only temporary in the continuing flow of transformation that is the nature of reality. Play it cool and you will play a better game. After you have matured a bit more you may even find the game to be amusing. Who needs other spectator sports when one can watch and participate in the moves and countermoves of the game of living? Of course you should do your very best to win. Give it all that you have. But learn to do so without the desperate fantasies of those who are unaware of the truth of our existence. Your opponents may think that all goodness is dependent upon them. You, by contrast, know that all goodness is secure in the power of the Self of the Universe.

Such gentle cynicism toward daily interpersonal competitive struggles may shock the righteous. Let them be shocked. That is their role in life. Let us play our part in the drama seriously while respecting those with different assignments. Let us oppose extreme evil with passionate dedication. And let us remember that all is finally well in the ultimate control of the One who creates conflict. He makes evil a real but ever subordinate challenge to the good. In the long run he sees to it that the darkness does not extinguish the light. At least he hasn't let that happen up to now, so it seems a bet worth making.

AFTER PLAYING YOUR PART

The child's question, "Where do you go when you die?" is perfectly natural within a child's way of understanding. It was a natural question, too, during the childhood of mankind hundreds of years ago and on up to the beginning of our age of new understanding of the nature of reality. As informed adults of our time, however, we know that such a question really doesn't apply to the situation. It is like asking, "Where does the television picture go when you turn off the set?" The fact is that the picture doesn't go anywhere. It is still present in the energy streaming from the broadcasting station.

Here again the metaphor of the relation between an actor and his role may assist our understanding. When the actor, John Smith, plays the role of Hamlet, he doesn't somehow split himself off from his own being. He remains John Smith. But while playing the role of Hamlet, John Smith voluntarily accepts the limitations of the words, actions, and feelings that are written as the role of Hamlet in the play. After the final curtain, Hamlet doesn't have to "go" somewhere to return to John Smith. Neither does the TV picture have to "go" somewhere to return to the field of broadcast energy. Nor does a person who dies have to "go" somehwere to return to the limitless Self of the Universe. In terms of our essential reality there is no need for us to travel anywhere. We simply step out of a particular role in the drama of history and by leaving these limitations we become again what we always were—the personal, living, infinite Self of the Universe.

In a contemporary understanding of the nature of reality, the human body is known to be a process taking place within the total continuum of the environment. In a previous analogy we spoke of the body as being like a whirlpool within the flowing water of a stream. Such a vortex is formed by some disturbance of the usual flow of current and it fades away after the disturbance is removed. A whirlpool may thus be formed by the stroke of a canoeist's paddle in the water. When the shaping and generative energy of the stroke of the paddle is removed, the whirlpool continues on for a while before the form dissipates.

Similarly, when the formative energy of the Self of the Universe is no longer active in the role of a particular human being at death, some aspects of that particular energy system remain in a space/time form for a while as they slowly disappear into other forms of existence. The body of the one who has died is an echo, an afterglow, a spatial memory that is sustained for a brief period after the shaping and sustaining power has been withdrawn. But this "withdrawal" is not a departure in the sense of a movement from one location to another. Rather, it is more like wakening from a dream of some kind of confined existence to a reality so vast and glorious that no words could possibly describe it. The finite is unable to comprehend the infinite. We have only one certainty: because the finite you is a differentiated form of the infinite Self of the Universe, your life is eternal. You are not a separate spark that could disappear in the dark. You are the self-expression of the Creating Power and you are eternal in his eternity. As John Smith does not die in the death of Hamlet, so you do not die in the death of your present embodiment. Whatever we may say beyond that simple certainty is the work of imagination motivated by enduring human desires and guided by rational probabilities.

A basic, durable human desire is the wish for a continuation of limited individuality after death. Our only experience of value is within space/time limitations. Everything we prize, all that makes life worthwhile, has come to us through our relationships with other limited forms of existence, and particularly through our relationships with other persons. It is to be expected that we find it impossible to imagine happiness apart from those we love.

An ancient Indian epic poem called the *Mahabharata* gives beautiful expression to this eternal longing for those we love. It tells of a hero who, having made the long pilgrimage to the place of final bliss, steps inside to find that "Heaven" is populated only by his enemies. He asks where he may find his friends and his family and he is told that they are all in "Hell." So he says that he, too, will go to the place of eternal torture, since no place could be Heaven for him without the presence of those he loves. He is led, then, to the terrible region of torment and he unhesitatingly enters. Whereupon the terrors vanish and he finds himself once again at the gate of Paradise. Inside he is able to see all of the people whom he loves, but still he is not allowed to enter. There is one more test. By his side is his faithful dog who has made the long pilgrimage with him, and he is told that dogs are forbidden to enter the place of final blessedness. Again he refuses to enter, for he will not abandon his canine friend. Whereupon the gates open wide, he is told that all living things are welcome, and he and his dog run joyfully to the arms of those they love.

That ancient Indian narrative expresses a universal human feeling that heaven would not be Heaven without the presence of those we love, and particularly without our most dearly beloved. Bliss cannot be experienced in isolation—or at least, so it seems to us within our space/time limitations. Furthermore, if final blessedness includes the completion of that which was left incomplete in the short years of our life on earth, then we may hope for continued individual identity. So many of our dearest hopes do not come true, and through no fault of our own. So much of our personal potential was not realized because of circumstances beyond our control. All of us tend to feel that this life always stops short of fulfillment, and it is only natural to want more—another chance, a further opportunity.

It is entirely reasonable to trust that there will be some further extension of personal individuality in the continuation of life after death. Instead of simply waking to our essential reality as the limitless Self of the Universe we could continue to play our familiar role on a new stage with further opportunities for adventure and growth. If the Creating Power can become you as a role in one drama, there is no intrinsic reason why he could not continue playing that part in another drama, or perhaps in a later act of this particular space/time production. Perhaps our moment of leaving the stage in Act One is simultaneous with making our entrance in Act Two. Indeed, when we think about such possibilities, it is not difficult to imagine that our present embodied existence may be Act 500 of our participation in the drama. Nor is there any necessity to confine our ideas to the stage of our familiar scene. The possibilities of future existence in other universes that vibrate on other wave-lengths are infinite.

In thus making such tentative flights of the imagination I find myself reluctant to be enthusiastic lest I appear to be opening the door to all kinds of "occult" foolishness: haunted houses, spooks, voices that communicate from the dead, mediums who describe life on the other side, claims that previous incarnations can be remembered under the influence of hypnotism—all of the chicanery by which the clever prey on the gullible. I will not deny that there may be a seed of truth in any or all of these claims, but the seeds are cultivated into mighty trees by devotees of the occult, and it has been my experience that some mighty strange birds are to be found nesting in the branches.

However, in thus expressing my doubts about the occult, I want to make it clear that I am not including the phenomena of extrasensory perception. Since reality is a single, seamless ocean of living power in which human beings (and all other things) exist as differentiations of the whole, it is obviously not impossible that an event in any one part of the system could affect some other "distant" part of the system.

I am personally persuaded that there is such a phenomenon as unconscious telepathic communication. I am convinced that it has happened, for example, that a person in Baltimore, Maryland, suddenly became vividly aware that a dear relative had just died in Greece—such awareness arriving at the exact moment of the relative's death, as the fact is later confirmed by normal methods of communication. I am certain, too, that lovers who care for one another with great intensity have an awareness of each other in many experiences of their life that goes beyond the use of our normal five senses. They are like poles of the same magnet, and they are sometimes in touch in non-verbal ways when miles of space separate them on the earth's surface. These, and other phenomena of parapsychology, are not impossible in our modern view of the nature of the universe as differentiations of a single dynamic whole. Each of us will decide for himself what claims of research of spontaneous experience he will accept. My personal feeling is that the whole field needs to be studied with a good deal of healthy skepticism because of the danger of being taken in by fakes and charlatans.

With that warning, then, we can go on to repeat the assertion that since the Self of the Universe has projected himself in the limited form which is your embodied being, there is no inherent reason why he could not continue the role in another part of the drama of the universe. Indeed, more people have believed in such a possibility of life after death than in any other idea of what may await us after this life is over. A wide variety of ideas of "reincarnation" has been part of almost all of the great religions other than Judaism and Christianity.

People of this persuasion point out that their belief helps

make sense out of life. It explains, for example, the existence of the child-genius. The musician who, at the age of twelve, composes music that is among the world's best, is a person who has had long experience with music in other incarnations. The doctrine also explains the birth of a deformed or retarded child, because the total condition of anyone's birth is the self-chosen result of the law of consequences, which is as much a built-in part of the universe as is the law of gravity. The most common name for this personal cause-and-effect sequence is the law of *karma*.

The best aid I know in interpreting the way the law of *karma* works is to imagine a man playing a hand of cards at the bridge table. He has thirteen cards to play, and there is no way that he can change the cards that he holds. Those thirteen may make up a very good bridge hand or a very poor one. If the hand is poor, the player is limited in what he can do with it. Nevertheless, a good player will get more out of a poor hand than will a duffer.

Now imagine that each time the man plays a card well in this particular hand of the total game he is, without being aware of it, dealing himself a better card for the next hand. When he plays a card poorly he has unconsciously dealt himself a lower card for the next hand. When his thirteen cards have all been played, he picks up his next hand, which is either better or worse than the one he has just finished playing, and in either case it is the hand that he unwittingly dealt himself by the choices he made in his previous hand.

Such is the law of *karma* or consequences. Your present life situation, with all of its limitations and opportunities, came to you neither as a punishment nor as a reward, for no supernatural judge sits over you and decides your fate. *Karma* is a natural law like Newton's laws of motion.

According to such teaching, the child born with severe physical handicaps is in a self-chosen situation. But even a poor hand can be played well. We are not able to judge, for example, what would be involved in playing well the role of a brain-damaged child. Yet it is not inconceivable that such a life might be lived well or poorly. Thus there is always the open opportunity to move upward in the order of reincarnation so that one may eventually become a person with such inborn goodness and wisdom that one's life is a blessing to all who know one. Those who interpret this life in terms of the doctrine of reincarnation will often speak of such a person as an "old soul," meaning one who has been on pilgrimage for a very long time and who has learned a great deal before arriving at this incarnation.

Yet it is interesting to note that Oriental philosophers generally do not think of the final goal as one of continual reincarnation in the form of a supremely good and wise person. Their hope of final consummation is to escape the process of reincarnation by returning to complete identification with the Creating Power. At the highest level or rebirth one has the possibility of awakening to one's true reality as the Self of the Universe. Thus being freed from the constrictions of the limited roles played in various reincarnations, the liberated person is in eternal, conscious union with all the good. Having become the Self of the Universe he will know all tears in laughter, all suffering in joy, darkness made glorious in light. No finite mind can truly describe such fulfillment. Hindu teachers use three words that hang in the air like notes of a silver bell: *sat, chit, ananda*. These are sounds on our side that mean *existence, consciousness, bliss*. The reality toward which they point is ineffable.

In the mood of reasonable speculation that feels to me as if it were a logical extrapolation of our experience of maturation in this life, I have wondered on some occasions whether our manifest longing for continued individuality in the company of others whom we love may be an indication that we have not yet reached the level of growth in which one may be liberated from rebirth. Our desire for continued bodily presence is a desire for life within limitations that kindle suffering as well as happiness. We will not transcend such finite existence until we come to the realization that what we really want is to know our true identity as the whole rather than as a subordinate activity of the whole. By living our present life well, we will grow in the capacity to experience such a desire.

If I were asked the standard by which one may measure whether or not one is living well in one's present incarnation, I would say that it is found in continuing growth in one's capacity to love.

Love is an inclusive kind of awareness. Genuine love is never "We two, Baby, and to hell with everyone else." When two people genuinely love one another their love spills over into affectionate relationships with all around them. The more intense their love, the wider their capacity to care for others. Since these others are various embodiments of the one Self of the Universe, this feeling of identification with an ever-widening circle of others is equivalent to an ever-increasing identification with the Creating Power. Projecting such growth beyond this life one could imagine the circle of a person's love becoming more and more inclusive until the love at last becomes boundless. Having thus burst the bonds, realization of the identity of self with the limitless Self is complete.

The reverse is also possible. One may so diminish in one's capacity to love that finally there is no love left—no awareness of identity with any other and hence no sense of identity with the One. The consequence then might be simply the disappearance of that "role" from the drama of the universe. But note this paradox: such loss of a particular role in the play would be a return to identification with the infinite One just as much as would the expansion of that role to limitless being by growth in love. No matter what may be the grounds for John Smith to stop playing the role of Hamlet, his own reality as a person is untouched. The role of any human being may be diminished by lack of love into nothing, or it may be expanded by growth in love into everything. Either results in

cessation of limited living and awakening to the limitless life
of the Creating Power. The only difference is that one path to
the final consummation is through the ever-increasing darkness of hostility while the other path is through ever-increasing light of loving. Such a distinction may not be enough to
satisfy those who long for the eternal torture of their enemies,
but we need not be much concerned with those who lust for
vengeance. Their understanding has not yet been much il-
lumined by carnal knowledge.

A better objection to the teaching of reincarnation according to the law of consequences is the assertion that if the
circumstances of this life are the result of our way of living
in a previous life, then the sick, the poor, the losers, are only
getting their just desserts. They are paying for previous wickedness, so it would seem to be right and proper to let them
suffer. The doctrine cuts the motivation for deeds of kindness
toward unfortunate people.

One should remember, however, that whatever may be the
cause of the condition of the needy, one's own future destiny
is dependent upon the practice of loving kindness. Suffering
may be self-chosen, but we will be choosing the same or worse
if we ignore it.

When we reach that point in imaginative ideas about future
life, we may realize that we are saying things like the old "be
good or else . . ." doctrine in which virtue was encouraged by
threats of damnation. We know the fallacy of such thinking.
Attempts to see beyond our finite horizon eventually run out
into absurdity.

Ideas about reincarnation and the law of *karma* are only
one kind of mythological thinking about life beyond. There
are others. All of them, as I have said, express the heart's longing for fulfillment of what was missing in this life and for a
continuation of the relationship of love with those who have
meant most to us. Since all such intuitive metaphors deal with
material beyond the reach of our knowing, there is no way to

prove any of them false. We can say, of this or that teaching, only that it seems improbable in view of what we already know about reality.

The one thing I am certain of is that death is only a transition. It may be to a continuing extension of our present individual role, or it may be to an awakening as the Self of the Universe. Because I love this life, because so many people, animals, birds, places and things are very dear to me, I am in no hurry to discover what awaits beyond. I am certain only that it is not annihilation, the total extinction of the self. I am not afraid. My confidence arises out of both carnal and intellectual knowledge of my eternal relationship with the Self of the Universe. My hope is that some of my readers, in their own way and using their own symbols of understanding, may equally grow so that they, too, can face the final curtain of their life with confident expectation.

THREE SERMONS

Miracles

Sermon preached by the Reverend Alfred B. Starratt in Emmanuel Church, Baltimore, the fifth Sunday after Easter, April 30, 1978 and over WBAL-AM, Radio 1090, May 7, 1978

My topic this morning is miracles. Because we are very familiar with Bible stories we may not realize the extent to which supernatural magic is central in all of these ancient narratives. Think of Moses holding up his arm and thus causing the Red Sea to separate and leave a dry pathway for the people of Israel to escape the Egyptians. Remember Elijah—how he could prevent the rain from falling; how he made the amount of flour in one small jar and the amount of oil in another to be endlessly renewed to provide food for himself and his friends; or how he brought a dead child back to life. I remind you also of the many miracles of Jesus—how he fed more than five thousand people on magically replenished portions of only two loaves of bread and five fish and gave all of them so much that there were twelve baskets of bread and fish left over after everyone had eaten all they could hold! We are told that he not only could walk on water, but that he could manage to do so when the surface was heaving and tossing in the wind. He raised a man from the dead and he himself was raised from the dead by God. Similar wonder tales appear in all biblical narratives.

Now if I asked you to tell me what a miracle is I think that most of you, as people of the twentieth century, would tell me that a miracle is any event that is contrary to what we know of natural law. We understand natural law to be a collection of brief scientific statements that describe how the universe be-

162

haves. The most common law of nature known to all of us is the one that we call the law of gravity. It describes the fact that any two bodies in space will be attracted to each other with a force that is directly proportional to the product of their masses and inversely proportional to the square of the distance between them. This is called a law of nature because it describes something that always happens. We can count on it. Hence we can predict with certainty the movement of the planets around the sun, for example. All of our scientific technology depends upon that kind of predictable order in nature. Because of it we can make an automobile or we can send people to the moon. The basic orderliness of the universe is the foundation assumption of all science. Scientific explanations of events are explanations that are derived from natural laws—from descriptions of what always and everywhere happens. So when an event happens that has no connection with previous experience—an event that science cannot explain because it goes contrary to natural law, then that event is called a miracle. That is the modern way of thinking about miracles. But let me remind you that no one in the ancient world ever thought of miracles as events that go contrary to natural law, for the simple reason that no one in the ancient world had ever heard of natural law. The people who wrote and who first read the biblical narratives were either animists or just a stage beyond animism. In other words, they were people who explained all movement in their environment as due to the choice and the will power of some invisible spirit— just as the movement of a man's body is due to the decision and will power of the man's invisible spirit. In their view of the world, things generally happen in predictable ways because spirits, like people, are creatures of habit and for the most part they act in old familiar patterns. A miracle, then, in their view of the world, has to be an event in which one spirit causes another spirit to behave in an unusual way. Thus, a miraculous event is the result of a dominant spirit commanding the behavior of a weaker and more submissive spirit. Moses had in him the powerful spirit of Yahweh, so he could command the water spirit to divide the waters. Jesus also had the spirit of Yahweh and he could command a storm god to stop making bad weather, so that in place of high wind and waves an immediate calm fell upon the sea. This, then, was the central meaning of miracles for people in the ancient world. For them, the miraculous was not a strange event that goes contrary to natural law. For them, a miracle is a sign of the presence and activity of some invisible spirit who can force other spirits to do something different. The most powerful of such commanding spirits was believed by biblical writers to be Yahweh, the god of the people of Israel.

Now one of the unfortunate things about invisible spirits is that you can't examine them—you can't get to know them in the same way that you can get to know another human being. Since you can't see Yahweh you have to infer what he is like by observing what he does—and what Yahweh does is mostly revealed in miracles—in the places where he intervenes in the usual order of things and makes his presence known by demanding the unexpected. So if you look at the miracle stories, what kind of god do you think of as the one who causes the biblical miracles?

In my opinion the miracle stories show a god who demonstrates special care for his friends, for people who please him, for the people he likes, and who shows indifference and at times malevolence toward all the rest. If you please him and he likes you, he will kill your enemies, and he will rescue you from pain and death. He will not only rescue you from starvation—he will also provide a lunch that is more than you could possibly eat in order to save you the inconvenience of going home to get some food. He will arrange the weather to suit your wishes and save you from tiresome boat rides by enabling you to walk on water.

This biblical god of miracles is thus a very powerful god who can do anything you want—but he won't lift a finger unless you are among those who have somehow won his favor. It seems to me that the miracle stories told by people in the ancient world imply that Yahweh is like a mighty monarch sitting on a magnificent throne in heaven where he can see all that is happening on the earth. People come crawling to him to beg favors because he rules not by some kind of general law, but rather, rules by personal caprice. And nothing pleases this arbitrary ruler more than submissive conformity to his slightest command. If he says, "Eat worms," you gobble them down. You wear a brass ring in your nose if you think he wants you to. Be endlessly obedient, but also be endlessly flattering to the violent old gentleman. Tell him over and over again how great he is, how much you admire him, how he has it all over other gods, praise him—and perhaps you will get to be one of his special people. And if you do, then not only will miracles be done for you, but you may even be given the power to do miracles for the benefit of your friends, and for the destruction of your enemies.

It seems to me that that is the kind of god that is implied by the miracle stories in the Bible, and the plain fact is that such a picture of god is no longer appealing or convincing to intelligent and thoughtful people of our time. Mind you, it's not all that is said about the biblical god, for the Bible is not a single, consistent document with only one understanding of god. The Bible is a library that covers a long period of human experience. It includes both the childishly primitive and the sublime. But God the miracle-worker is not, as I see it, one of the sublime ways of thinking about the deity.

In modern theology, God is not one spirit among many, who shows his might by commanding the others and forcing their obedience for the benefit of his friends and the confounding of the enemies of his friends. In modern theology God is beyond all possible definition because he is without beginning and without end, and everything that now exists, that ever has existed, or that ever will exist is a form of his being. Such a truly infinite and all-inclusive God cannot be partisan, for every person on both sides of every dispute is, so to speak, a role played by the limitless God. The rejoicing of the victor is his. The suffering of the vanquished is his. Every life is a form of his boundless life. He does not play favorites.

Neither does the infinite God rule by personal whim or caprice. He expresses himself in the basic order of the universe because such order is a necessary basis for freedom. Without order freedom is merely chaos. Order creates a dependable frame of reference within which meaningful choices can be made. When driving an automobile I am free to step on the brake or to step on the gas, but that freedom is meaningful only to the degree that I can predict the consequences of my choice. Without the dependable order that makes such prediction possible my freedom is meaningless. So this God-in-everything is a God of both dependable order and unpredictable freedom. He is orderly in nature and free in people.

And even in nature this infinite God is not bound by iron necessity. The laws of nature are descriptions of the general order of the universe, but it is a statistical order, that is, an order based upon probability. Contemporary quantum theory tells us that there is an element of the unpredictable at the very heart of its theoretical structure of reality. Thus events that are contrary to past experience *can* happen, and such unexpected occurrences are what modern people mean when they speak of a miracle.

One practical question remains. In the ancient world it was believed that by submissive obedience, continuous praise and constant, believing supplication in prayer, you could win the favorable attention of Yahweh and get him to work miracles for you. Is there anything similar to this in a modern way of thinking about God?

I believe that there is. I believe that the religious person in our time can generate miracles—not as special favors granted by a partisan King of the Universe, but rather by having developed such sensitivity to the divine presence and activity in the world that he can, so to speak, tune in to possibilities unknown to most people. The general run of human beings are blown in the direction followed by the winds of necessity. The religious person is like the skillful skipper of a modern sailboat who can use the power of the wind to go in a direction opposite to that in which the wind is blowing. Or, to use another analogy, the modern religious person may be likened to a receiving apparatus that is sensitive to wave lengths of energy vibration that are continuously present but unknown to most people who are not tuned to that particular channel. In other words, the modern religious person can develop a capacity for doing the unexpected because he is aware of a wider range of the constant activity of God than is the average man or woman. He is tuned into powers unknown to others and can use them to produce miracles.

I'm obviously dealing here with events that I do not completely understand, but my intuition tells me that in our modern world the religious person who can work miracles is one who has discovered in personal experience that all creation is the self-expression of God—one who can feel the divine presence in all forms of existence—one who, therefore, feels a continuing sense of unity between himself and all the others —in other words, a person with a capacity for all-inclusive loving. The more ability one has to feel what the other person or animal is feeling, the more compassion one has for all living things; equally the more unusual will be one's ability to use the power of God in constructive and creative ways. The religious man in the modern world is one who loves God in all that is around him and who thus shares to a much more than ordinary degree in both the divine pleasure and the divine pain in all that happens anywhere. He feels the sorrows and suffering of others, but there is a light that shines in the darkness and the darkness cannot overcome it. The evil is real but it exists only to make the good possible and it can never finally conquer the good. So the person who is sensitive to God, while feeling compassion, will generally be a joyous person. You will hear him or her praising God—not as a religious obligation and not in an attempt to win divine favor by flattery, but rather as the spontaneous expression of a grateful heart. He or she will be thankful to the Self of the Universe and the thankfulness will come out in the kind of praise that sings with delight—as in the lovely song called "Oh, What a Beautiful Mornin' " in the musical, "Oklahoma!"

I think that all of us are more aware of the possibility of miracles when our mood is high and we are sensitive to the beauty of God in all creation. That's when miracles can be believed in. That's when miracles can happen. That's when they *do* happen. The universal lover cares for what is happening to the other and his caring calls forth unexpected transformations in events—his loving opens the way for extraordinary expressions of the power of God.

As I see it, then, many (perhaps most) of the miracle stories in the Bible are pious fiction rather than records of fact. But some of them are narratives derived from real events in history. Primitive people had a childish understanding of such events and of God. Similarly a primitive person brought into our culture might think that flipping an electric light switch summons a genie to give light to the room. His explanation is wrong, but the light still comes on when he flips the switch. From our twentieth-century viewpoint the biblical way of explaining miracles was in error, but despite such misunderstanding, miracles continued to happen. In our time we can come to understand that people who are sensitive to God through love illuminated by reason are often surrounded and protected by extraordinary events, and often they are able to use that same living power for the benefit of others. Such a way of thinking about miracles makes sense to me and I have found it confirmed in experience. I hope that the same may be true for you.

Providence or Chance?

Sermon preached by the Reverend Alfred B. Starratt in Emmanuel Church, Baltimore, on Pentecost 18, September 17, 1978 and over WBAL-AM, radio 1090, September 24, 1978

Our topic today is "Providence or Chance?" and we begin with three statements:

(1) "When Ehud died, once again the Israelites began to do what displeases Yahweh, and Yahweh handed them over to Jabin, king of Canaan, who reigned at Hazor."

(2) "Think of the flowers. They never have to spin or weave, yet I assure you that not even Solomon in all his regalia was robed like one of these. Now if that is how God clothes the grass in the field which is there today and thrown into the furnace tomorrow, how much more will he look after you, you men of little faith!"

(3) "When I have planned to do something, and some unforeseen event or circumstance prevents me from doing it, I always feel that God has prevented me for some very good reason."

The first of these three statements is from the Book of Judges—a book in which the author writes history as a record of the way in which God punished his people for disobedience and rewarded them for conformity to his will. There can be no doubt that the author of the book of Judges believed that the large events of history are controlled by God.

The second quotation is from Jesus of Nazareth who was not concerned with the rise and fall of kingdoms, but who equally believed that God can control events of history in such a way as to express loving care for those who seek to do his will.

The third quotation is from a twentieth-century religious person, namely, my wife. I asked her what she thought about the doctrine of providence and she answered by saying, "When I have planned something and then I can't do it, I always feel that God made the project impossible for a good reason."

The doctrine of providence, then, is one of the oldest and more durable of religious ideas. To believe in providence is to believe that God can, and often does, control the events of history in order to help his friends and harm his enemies. In the biblical books the idea of being punished by divine providence is just as strongly stated as is the idea of being rewarded, and it is not completely forgotten in modern times. Many of us have smiled when Maude, on television, says to her husband, "God will get you for that, Walter." We don't really expect that the Almighty will play the part of a "hit man" for our personal need of retribution. Yet when disaster overtakes one whom we judge to be wicked we are not above considering the event to be punishment arranged by God.

It is, however, the positive side of the doctrine that most of us seem to find appealing. People tend to attribute to the providence of God any event that provides an unexpectedly happy outcome through circumstances that were contrary to our personal will or beyond our individual control. We thank God when we miss our plane and then hear that it crashed on landing. If you were in need of money and you were forced to sell your patent for a new kind of horseshoe just before Henry Ford came out with his Model T and everyone began buying automobiles, you would very likely be grateful to God for his providential care. So the question we are dealing with this morning is this: Does God occasionally manage the events of history in such a way as to support and protect individuals or groups or nations? Are happy events ever divinely arranged or are they the product of pure chance?

Two kinds of people would attribute happy outcomes to chance: Those who believe there is no God, and those who believe that there is a God who once upon a time created the universe as a vast machine, so ordered that it would evolve into the forms we now see around us, but that having created such a machine the divine engineer went off to work on other projects and he now has nothing to do with human history. Atheists and Deists (pronounced "DEEists") would reckon good or ill fortune to be the result of chance—the unpredictable, unintentional falling-together of a particular set of cause and effect relationships. They would deny that there is any spy in the sky keeping an eye on events among men. We're all familiar with the lines written by James Russell Lowell, in "The Present Crisis":

> Though the cause of evil prosper, yet 'tis truth alone is strong,
> Though her portion be the scaffold and upon the throne be wrong.
> Yet that scaffold sways the future, and, behind the dim unknown,
> Standeth God within the shadow, keeping watch above his own.

The atheist and the deist would deny that God thus watches the defeat of the good and out of the ashes builds an even better tomorrow. He hasn't really "got the whole world in his hand" and he hasn't got "you and me, brother, in his hand." Sigmund Freud thought that some men and women never outgrow their need of parents, so after the death of their own mother and father they imagine a big Daddy or Mommy in the sky. As the writer of the ancient philosophical poem that we call the Book of Job clearly saw, good men can be destroyed in agony and wicked men can prosper in good health. Though Jesus of Nazareth is quoted as being confident that God will care for the needs of those who seek to live in obedience to his will, he is also quoted as reminding his followers that God sends rain and sunshine equally upon the just and the unjust—no special favors for the good. When any one of us looks at the uneven distribution of desirable things in this life it seems much easier to consider the situation to be the result of chance rather than the result of divine providence. It seems easier to see our world as the result of mindless energy rather than as the product of divine intelligence. It seems easier to be an impersonalist than to be a personalist in one's way of understanding the universe and the events of history.

In answering such arguments I must begin by reminding you that I am a Panentheist. That is, I am one who takes seriously the infinity of God. I am persuaded that what we call a universe is a name for an activity of God in the same way that a smile is a name for an activity of a face. The universe and everything in it is the self-expression of God and all of it is identical with God. The universe is God, but at the same time God is more than this or any other universe that we could possibly imagine. That is the difference between a pantheist and a panentheist. A pantheist sees this universe as the self-expression of God, but he doesn't think of God as transcending this universe. He says only (as the name of his philosophy expresses it), "All is God." The Pane*n*theist, on the other hand, says, "All is God and all is *in* God." In other words, God is *more* than his local activity as our universe.

Now if God is the Self of the Universe—if the universe is the manifestation of God in the same way that my visible bodily presence is the manifestation of my personal self—then the doctrine of providence cannot be completely wrong, but neither is the usual way of thinking about it completely correct.

It is certainly true, for example, that as a personal self I experience free will and some of my actions are the result of deliberate choice—but not all of them. Many of my actions are simply habitual and are done without thought or choice. Then, in addition, my personal being includes a whole biochemical system of mechanistic or electronic activity—a cause-and-effect system that is related to the conscious states of my personal existence, but yet can be well-described in impersonal terms. Thus a personal self includes (1) direct personal choice, (2) indirect personal choice described as habit, and (3) impersonal activities of a biochemical kind that can be described as a mechanistic or electronic system.

By analogy, then, one would expect that within nature as a manifestation of the Self of the Universe, there would be occasions of personal choice plus continuities that correspond to habitual activities, plus an underlying ground of relatively impersonal electronic and mechanistic systems. It seems to me that this is precisely what one finds in the world around us. There is the relatively impersonal aspect of things studied by scientists. There are the great continuities that are like habits and that gradually change as in the slow process of evolution. Then there are occasions of particular personal control or choice made by God. The doctrine of providence applies to these latter events—the events that are the result of directly willed action by the Self of the Universe.

I argue, then, that it is not irrational to believe that there could be occasions of divinely willed activity in the course of our human experience, but I would also argue that there is no empirical evidence that compels such belief, and I don't see how there could be. In order to prove that a particular event happened because the Self of the Universe directly and consciously chose to make it happen that way, one would need to have direct and indisputable knowledge of the mind of God, and I think that that is impossible for us in our present limited human state of existence.

On the other hand, however, I remind you that I have no way to prove that some activity of any one of my human friends is a consequence of conscious choice, for I cannot get inside of another human mind any more than I can get inside of the mind of God.

Yet I am aware that some of my actions are the result of conscious choice and I am intuitively aware that your mind is not unlike my own. Hence I am certain, by intuition rather than by provable empirical evidence, that like me you often act out of free conscious choice. In the same way there are occasions when some of us feel a personal element in the circumstances and events that surround and shape our personal life, and we intuitively thank God for unexpected beneficial outcomes.

As a Panentheist, therefore, I feel that there is a substratum of impersonal mechanistic and electronic control of most of what happens in nature. Above that basic level there are cyclic and repetitive continuities with slow change—continuities that are like the force of habit in my own personal life. And above that level I am persuaded that there is an area of conscious divine control of events. Without this latter I cannot explain how the universe evolved into the world we now see around us or how you and I evolved out of starfire. For me it requires a far greater act of faith to ascribe the existence of human beings to blind and mindless chance than it does to say that we are the result of the conscious intent of a mind infinitely superior to our own.

My argument shows that it is possible that some events may be providential but it gives no proof that any one particular event is so. It is probable that people will see the hand of God in some set of circumstances that was really only the chance arrangement of the mechanical aspects of nature. People will often mistakenly believe that they are being rewarded or punished by God. But there are times when circumstances truly express the direct conscious control of the Self of the Universe. It *can* happen, and I think that the best judge of when and where it is happening is the kind of person who is most sensitively aware of the personal presence of God in the world around us—the person who responds in love to animals, to trees, birds, flowers, stars, clouds, oceans, all the beauty and wonder of this lovely universe. If I were looking for a person to tell me what events were acts of divine providence and what events were not, I would choose St. Francis of Assisi rather than Adolf Hitler. I would trust poets rather than politicians, and lovers rather than church officials. I'll trust Emily Dickenson, who wrote,

> I never saw a moor,
> I never saw the sea,
> Yet know I how the heather looks,
> And what a wave must be.
>
> I never spoke with God,
> Nor visited in Heaven,
> Yet certain am I of the spot
> As if the chart were given.

Let us pray: Thou who are nearer than breathing, closer than hands and feet, so much one with us that we cannot know you as an object among other objects on the far side of our sensory apparatus; help us, we pray, to find your presence in all things by knowing our kinship with all creation; that being aware of you we may live with confidence that all that happens to us can never take us from thee. We ask it in Christ's name. Amen.

Why Pray for Others?

Sermon preached by the Reverend Alfred B. Starratt in Emmanuel Church, Baltimore, the nineteenth Sunday after Pentecost, September 24, 1978 and over WBAL-AM, radio 1090, October 1, 1978

Near our vacation place in Chester, Nova Scotia, there is a Provincial Park called Graves Island where we go almost every evening to take our two poodles for a walk. One day last summer we were surprised to find hundreds of swallows gathered in the Park. The fields and trees were filled with them and the air was thick with them like some great swarm of insects. The flock stayed there for two days and then it vanished. The experience made me read a bit about migrating birds and I learned that some of them fly thousands of miles from the northern to the southern hemisphere and they return to the same location at both ends of their migratory journey every year. How do they do it? How do they pinpoint the exact location where they were the previous years after flying over several thousand miles of land and ocean? Scientists have made some guesses, but no one really knows. Something leads them home year after year.

It's like salmon. They can wander through the waters of the world, but when the time comes they go right back to the little inland brook where they were born. Scientists think that it may have something to do with the water of the place where the fish were born. They wired a salmon to register on electrical gadgets when he was excited and then they exposed him to various batches of fresh water taken from many different places. Nothing happened until he was put in water from the pool of his birth, and then he lit up like a Christmas tree.

Some molecule in the fish's sensory apparatus was programmed to respond only to hometown water. But how does that molecule recognize the right water? And how does it trace that particular type of water through hundreds of miles of ocean water so that it can swim back to the right river and follow it up to the right brook and go up the right brook to the right pool?

Or to come to nearer and more familiar territory, what about the mystery of the construction of a human body? We know that the genes carry a blueprint, so to speak, but how do the new cells read the blue print? How does one cell know that its task is to be part of the liver while another receives orders to be part of an eyeball? Some kind of chemical communication goes from cell to cell or from some other commanding vibrations, but we don't know what or how.

When you are playing the game called scientific explanation, there are certain simple rules that you must follow: What you observe must be seen in relation to something we already know. You must report on it in simple language showing how it is related to present scientific knowledge. Your theory must be supported by being able to do it again or by predicting that it will happen again. You then have a sound scientific explanation. But there is a difference between sound scientific explanations and final truth. An old Egyptian astronomer named Ptolmey had a good scientific explanation for the apparent movement of stars and planets. He could predict when there would be an eclipse. But no one today follows Ptolemy's explanation. His theory was correct according to the rules but not true in any final sense.

J. Robert Oppenheimer, one of the greatest of modern scientists, wrote the following: "When a student of physics makes his first acquaintance with the theory of atomic structure and of quanta he must come to the rather deep and subtle notion which has turned out to be the clue to unraveling that whole domain of physical experience. This is the

178

notion of complimentarity, which recognizes that various ways of talking about experience may each have validity, and may each be necessary for the adequate description of the physical world, and yet may stand in mutually exclusive relationship to one another, so that in a situation to which one applies, there may be no consistent possibility of applying the other."

What this means is that reality is not a one-and-only set of principles. What we call "reality" depends upon what assumptions we choose, what rules of explanation we follow. The easy and natural thing for any one of us is to adopt the popular rules of explanation in our culture and make these the basis for our truth. Sooner or later we expect everything to conform to our notions, and what doesn't conform we would assert is simply not true.

In the opinion of most intelligent and well-educated modern men and women of our time and place, this universe is believed to be a collection of material objects related to one another by the laws of nature, and evolving into new forms by mindless chance. To their way of thinking it is impossible for cousin Mary to wake up in the night with an accurate feeling of certainty that Uncle Bill who lives five thousand miles away has just died. It is impossible that some intelligence guides a cell in building a whale, or that some intelligence guides birds and fish in their turning homeward. It is impossible that a guiding intelligence shapes the growth and destiny of all living things—that it has done so through all the years and all the transformations of evolutionary history from the very beginning. It is impossible that this universe is more like a mind than like a machine, more a single being than a collection of independent items, more intelligence than chance. And together with all these other impossibilities there is the one that scoffs at the idea of intercessory prayer. The mind of each person is believed to be locked up inside of his skull. The person can be aware of the world through the bodily senses and act upon the world through movements of the body—

period. There is no way that one person praying in one place can bring about changes in the physical condition of another person in a hospital several miles away.

People used to think that such a prayer could be effective because there is a God who lives above the sky and listens to the prayers of good people. This heavenly father has the power to work miracles and, having heard your prayer, he might decide to cure the illness of the person for whom you were praying. But in our day the benevolent old man who lives in the sky is no longer believable. Like Jupiter or Athena or Apollo, he has become a mythological figure—a character in ancient stories told by our ancestors. So the scientific impersonalist will believe that it is useless to pray for others.

Well, I don't agree. I'm willing to give two cheers for science and for scientific explanations of ourselves and our world. I do not want to make light of the amazing achievements of our great scientists. So much do I respect their methods and their work that I hesitate to criticize them and thus seem to open the door for all kinds of mindless and idiotic superstitions foisted upon the gullible by the credulous. Yet in all candor I must say that scientific explanations deserve no more than two cheers. I reserve the third, of three cheers, for those few scientists and philosophers who can pass beyond the barriers of scientific explanations and accept the possibility that the principle of complimentarity extends beyond theories about such things as the propagation of light as both waves and particles. The impersonal explanation of the universe as a gigantic electronic field or as a mechanical contrivance is true, but it is equally true that the universe is living, intelligent consciousness—a single paraorganic system —a union of many different forms within a single body similar to the unity of differences such as liver, bones, hair, brains, blood in a single human body. The visible and tangible universe is, so to speak, the body of God. He is the self that pervades, shapes, moves, brings forth and receives back all of the forms of existence. So I, in one part of his being, am aware of suffering in another part of his being, and I pray. My prayer is not just a flicker of electrical energy running around in the cells of my brain. My prayer is conscious life directed to a particular purpose—my prayer is a set of vibrations in the very structure of the one who is the inner life of all. It's vaguely like the brain sending a message to the hand—"Move! You dummy! You're touching a hot stove!" Only this is not, in most cases, such a powerful stimulus or command as a nerve impulse responding to the sensation of burning. It isn't usually as powerful—but it is *there*. It *is* real. One part of the body of God is interacting with another part of the body of God and it *can* make a difference if the interaction is strong enough.

Here there is no question of telling God something that he doesn't know. There is no question of trying to get the Almighty to grant you a favor, or to change his mind and make him merciful when he might have been unmindful of what was happening. There is no question of sending messages across empty space or of mind having some kind of magical effect upon matter.

In the paradigm we're talking about now, the whole of reality is living conscious energy. The universe is a single limitless ocean of intelligent, purposeful, creating power, and all that happens in it anywhere is experienced by the Self of the Universe just as I experience what happens in my body. A prayer that is an intense expression of loving concern for my friend in need is a conscious activity within the mind of God and it makes a difference—sometimes a difference so powerful that the transformation in my friend's condition seems almost miraculous.

And please note that such possibilities are open whether or not one correctly understands the way in which it happens. I may think that my prayer is granted by an old man who lives in the sky, or I may assume that Jesus or Mohammed or the

Buddha has been summoned as an invisible spirit by my prayer, or that I am the possessor of mysterious healing vibrations unknown to other persons. However I explain it, my intense loving concern, focused upon the need of my friend, can make a difference. It's like the ignorant person who thinks that an elf who lives in the refrigerator turns on the light each time the door is opened. Such an explanation is incorrect, but still the light goes on when the door is opened. So there are lots of mistaken notions about intercessory prayer, but such prayer can still have an effect when motivated by intense love from one time/space location in the body of God to another time/space location in the body of God.

Well, we started today with a minor natural mystery—how do some birds fly literally thousands of miles to southern homes below the equator and then return to the exact place in the north where they nested the year before? We noted other mysteries: the migration of salmon; the way that a single cell not only can know how to build a whale but can pass on the instructions and guide the other cells to assume the proper shape and function in the right place. We wondered about the intelligent power that guides the evolutionary process and still works within each of us as our fundamental life energy? I mentioned these mysteries to remind you that the rules of scientific explanation do not and cannot explain everything. Indeed, science itself has come to recognize that contrary and inconsistent assumptions are necessary to explain a world that doesn't fit together neatly as a single cause-and-effect system.

Then I called your attention to the picture of the universe as guided by a single intelligence—not externally by a God *outside* of the process, but rather, internally by a God who *is* the process while at the same time he transcends it, just as anything done by my hand is done by me, although I am far more than my hand. If the universe is, so to speak, the body of God, then the activity of prayer stimulated by loving concern for the need of a friend is something like a pain in the one part of my body stimulating an action to remove the pain. Intercessory prayer can make a real difference—even to the extent of what appears to be miraculous healing.

Let me close by saying that I really haven't "proved" anything by what I have said. I've only shared with you my thinking about why it is not unreasonable to pray for others. The first step in effective prayer is not to feel foolish in doing it—to understand the universe in such a way as to feel that it truly could make a difference. Perhaps my words will make such prayer easier for you when your love imparts a desperate urgency to help and there is nothing else that you can do. I sincerely hope so.

Let us pray:

Self of the Universe, life of our life and life of all that exists,
we ask to be more sensitive to your personal presence in
all things, that responding to you in love for all around us, we
may be led to realize possibilities for helping others that are
hidden from those whose minds are blocked by dogmatic
assumptions, beyond which they are unaware. We ask it in
the name of Christ, who reached beyond the thought-world
of his time to express love for a God who is infinite. Amen.

Led by constant sensitivity to a single Presence in all forms of existence, ALFRED B. STARRATT has lived his life on the far side of traditional habits of thought. Born in Quincy, Massachusetts, and educated in public schools, he graduated from Boston University, then from the Episcopal Theological School in Cambridge, and earned his Ph.D. from Harvard. Finding Oriental philosophies most congenial to mystical insight, he became a teacher at Huachung University in Central China. Upon returning to the United States after the Communist revolution, he took a parish in Stockbridge, Massachusetts, and then went on to teach at Kenyon College, Ohio. In 1955 he and his wife Anne, together with three daughters, came to Baltimore to revive Emmanuel Episcopal Church, in the central city, by gathering a congregation of people who find traditional theology no longer persuasive. Though primarily a teacher and pastor, he led the fight for equal-opportunity legislation in Maryland, and has been prominent in issues of family planning. Much of his parish visiting is done on his motorcycle, and the trophies in his library testify to his skill in racing sailboats. Among his radio listeners are Christians, Jews, Hindus, agnostics, the whole range of religious opinion. His philosophy is inclusive rather than exclusive. In thought and action, Dr. Starratt lives on the growing edge of tomorrow.

Designed by Barbara Holdridge

Cover design, title page and chapter opening line motifs by Mary Atherton.

Composed in Linotype Janson with Torino display
by the Maryland Linotype Composition Company,
Baltimore, Maryland

Printed on 60-pound Glatfelter Offset,
hardbound in Permalin Buckram Slate Gray and Wedgewood Blue,
and bound in paper by Fairfield Graphics,
Fairfield, Pennsylvania

Jacket and cover color separation by Capper, Inc.,
Knoxville, Tennessee

Jacket and cover printed by Rugby Associates, Inc.,
Knoxville, Tennessee